Safe Spaces, Brave Spaces

Safe Spaces, Brave Spaces

Diversity and Free Expression in Education

John Palfrey
Foreword by Alberto Ibargüen

The MIT Press
Cambridge, Massachusetts
London, England

This book was set in ITC Stone Serif Std by Toppan Best-set Premedia Limited. Printed and bound in the United States of America.

Library of Congress Cataloging-in-Publication Data

Names: Palfrey, John G. (John Gorham), 1972- author.
Title: Safe spaces, brave spaces : diversity and free expression in
    education / John Palfrey.
Description: Cambridge, MA : MIT Press, [2017] | Includes
    bibliographical references and index.
Identifiers: LCCN 2017008607 | ISBN 9780262037143 (hardcover : alk.
    paper)
Subjects: LCSH: Academic freedom--United States. | Freedom of speech--
    United States. | Multicultural education--United States. | Educational
    equalization--United States. | Teaching--Social aspects--United States.
Classification: LCC LC72.2 .P35 2017 | DDC 370.1170973--dc23 LC
    record available at https://lccn.loc.gov/2017008607

10 9 8 7 6 5 4 3 2 1

for Sean and Judy Palfrey
exceptional parents and
inspiring educators

Contents

Foreword

On March 2, 2017, conservative author Charles Murray gave a speech at Middlebury College. It ended in a near riot. Student activists argued that Murray's views had no place on campus. As they put it in a letter to the administration: "Racism under the guise of academic discourse is still racism"—and they wanted none of it.

Pundits declared the end of free speech. In the words of one cable news host, "On campus, you either have silent appeasement or a bruise." He went on to compare activists to cavemen.

This tribalization of public debate, which weaponizes terms like "dialogue" and "sensitivity," is at the heart of this timely book that should be as useful to school leaders as to editorial writers trying to understand what's happening on campuses.

In his examination of free speech debates on American college campuses, Palfrey asks readers a simple question: Must a community tolerate intolerance in the name of free expression? It's a question I thought my generation had answered. After the upheaval of the Second World War, America in the 1950s saw an unprecedented middle-class revival. With it came an emphasis on convention, tolerance of segregation in much of the country, blacklists, and fear of communism. You couldn't say or do many things on television; on sitcoms, married couples only had twin beds.

Cultural repression provokes creative response. The 1950s brought one of the great periods of dynamic and rebellious literature, painting, and dance in the country's history. The 1960s followed, with social and political upheaval for racial equality and women's rights and against the war in Vietnam—all openly and vehemently protested, freely televised, and extensively reported. As Berkeley activist Mario Savio put it, the only way to stop "the operation of the machine" was with unfettered speech, wholly consistent with the views of the Founding Fathers who, generations earlier, railed against their "machine," called England.

My generation's view of free speech was shaped by the Supreme Court's *The New York Times v. Sullivan* (1964), which held that you're free to write what you believe so long as there's no "actual malice." In broad strokes, it reaffirmed the founding principle that more speech is better than less.

You couldn't yell "Fire!" in a crowded theater and the standard for libel became malice but, short of that, you were pretty much free to express any viewpoint. That fed the pent-up anger over racial and gender injustice that exploded in the 1970s. Television morphing into cable and subscription services allowed speech rules to be relaxed. And then came the Internet, democratizing everything, achieving a kind of free speech Nirvana.

Our evolving understanding of community morphed from a culture of social convention and assimilation to one of respect and admiration for diversity. In time, inclusion became one of America's core values, worthy not just of encouragement but of protection.

And there's the rub: if a previous generation thought physical safety in a theater or one's reputation in a newspaper were worth protecting, this generation is adding inclusion and diversity to that vaunted level.

Students on campuses today are forcing us to consider that the physical harm that might come from yelling "Fire!" may be no less damaging than the scourge of racism. Each causes harm: one physical, the other emotional.

In the spirit of the First Amendment, let's hear these students out.

As Palfrey notes, students across the country are grappling with the legacy of the Founding Fathers. The framers declared the equality of mankind but reserved it for white men of means. It took centuries, a civil war, economic changes, constitutional amendments, courage, and tears for the principles to apply to everyone. So, is it any wonder that in the First Amendment, the part of the Constitution that touches all of us daily, many see a tool used for continued exclusion?

We mustn't let that be. We need to find the living, breathing extension of the founding ideal that diversity and free expression make for better democracy.

Students are not trying to abolish the First Amendment. Knight Foundation's 2016 Gallup survey of campus attitudes toward free speech found that 78 percent of students believed colleges should expose them to many viewpoints. What is challenging to an older generation is the treatment of diversity and inclusion as a value to be put up against unfettered speech, which led 69 percent of the large sample to favor restricting the use of slurs or language offensive to certain groups, which I interpret as "safe spaces."

These values must not be ignored. They aren't a fad. It is a young generation's response to society and should be understood as an evolving interpretation of free speech rights for the new millennium.

As ever in debate, some remedies may lack coherence or common sense. Should we stop teaching the Western canon because it is Eurocentric? Is an argument against safe spaces truly a form of hate speech? Is pulling a fire alarm a good way to prevent an intolerant speaker from having an audience?

The social psychologist Jonathan Haidt has noted that much of the free speech movement on campuses today has morphed into a "quasi-religion." It seeks to stamp out dissenting views as heresy and mobilizes social media rage to shame sinners into silence. This may sound dystopian and exaggerated, but for many professors and students on American college campuses, this ideological tightrope has become an everyday reality.

Palfrey explores both sides of the debate—sensitivity and inclusion on one hand, unfettered speech on the other—but refrains from reductive answers. He is a thoughtful head of school in search of workable solutions that uphold our founding value of free speech, balanced against other societal values, particularly those embraced by a younger generation.

Cool heads will prevail, he reasons, when we push back against factionalism with reasoned compromise and thoughtful debate. When a right-wing author is attacked at Middlebury, or a University of Chicago dean says he doesn't believe in trigger warnings, it feeds the culture of polarization, as does dismissing a generation as "snowflakes." We should move away from caricatures that reduce complex social issues into soundbites.

Is free speech in the late stages of entropy, or simply facing a speed bump? This book makes the case for the latter. In tracing the genealogy of this debate and suggesting mechanisms to move forward, *Safe Spaces, Brave Spaces* provides a worthy perspective on this crucial discussion.

Alberto Ibargüen
President, John S. and James L. Knight Foundation

Acknowledgments

This project began with an intention to write a scholarly article. I am grateful for the encouragement of Gita Manaktala and Amy Brand at MIT Press to expand the argument into this short book intended for an audience of educators. I am also grateful to acquisitions assistant Jesús J. Hernández, production editor Marcy Ross, copy editor Elizabeth Judd, and all those at MIT Press who collaborated with me on this project.

I have worked closely with Gosia Stergios on this project from the start, and owe her endless thanks for her partnership in this work. Her passion and hard work have made this a much better book than it otherwise would have been. Linda Carter Griffith has been my teacher and guide over the past five years at Andover, especially with respect to the essential work of diversity, equity, and inclusion. My colleagues in the Head of School's office at Andover—Melissa Dolan, Nancy Jeton, and Belinda Traub—have been essential to this project and to making possible all else I've been working on. Martha Minow, Jonathan Zittrain, Urs Gasser, and other friends at Harvard Law School have been wonderful teachers and guides with respect to many sides of the argument. I thank the four anonymous peer reviewers who gave thoughtful comments on the proposal and first draft; their constructive criticism has improved this book. Though we have not met, I am indebted to Ken Dautrich for his long-running work on the attitudes of young people toward free expression. Alberto Ibargüen and Sam Gill at the John S. and James L. Knight Foundation, along with Eric Newton (formerly at Knight and now at ASU), have supported essential research into the First Amendment and young people's views over the past decade, which is crucial to our understanding of these issues on campuses and in society at large. I am grateful for all the help I've received, from these friends and others.

As ever, my most enduring and deepest thanks go to my family. Any errors and omissions are mine alone.

1 Introduction

Safe spaces, trigger warnings, microaggressions, the disinviting of speakers, the demands to rename campus landmarks and symbols—each of these flashpoints has given rise to heated debates that have raged from lecture halls to the op-ed pages of the *Wall Street Journal* and the *New York Times* and reverberated in social media. A cottage industry has cropped up, in which writers tease student activists on blogs, in national newsmagazines, and in all manner of literature, deriding these young people as "crybullies" and "snowflakes" who feel the need to be protected by institutions from the harmful effects of life in a twenty-first-century democracy. The most serious of these critiques have merit, as student activists have had a tendency to overreach in calling for certain speech to be restricted in their zealousness for change and for a faster route to social justice. But many of the critiques are cheap shots that fail to inquire seriously into the claims of student activists. They tend to obscure valuable points about the importance of free expression and diversity, equity and inclusion. These critiques also ignore the strong support among the majority of students for free expression, free press, the right to assemble peaceably, and diversity that replicates the demographics of the world at large.

We will remember the academic years between 2014 and 2017 as times of turmoil on our campuses. Throughout the academic world, we have struggled to uphold our core values in the face of challenges from inside and outside our walls. This turmoil has taken the form of unrest on our campuses that has put a series of public debates—over race, class, sexual assault, the cost of education, climate change, and many other topics—into the forefront of intellectual discourse in our communities. The election cycle that vaulted Donald J. Trump to victory only exacerbated the tension and polarization of our nation with regard to these core issues. The increased risks facing students traveling from one country to another as a result of changing immigration policies have dampened enthusiasm for cross-cultural study. The pressure of addressing these concerns has occupied the minds of faculty and staff, as well as large numbers of students, as we go about the day-to-day business of teaching and learning.

The events of the past few academic years on many college campuses—including Yale, Missouri, DePaul, Middlebury, Berkeley, and Occidental, among many others—have pulled many of these divisive topics into public debate in ways that are both constructive and distorting. Social media has made matters yet more complex—mostly for the worse. Events that had previously remained localized affairs became national and international incidents, thanks to camera phones, Twitter, Facebook, and Snapchat. Hateful speech and the responses to it have spilled over from tiny campuses to the world at large. As these disputes are replayed over and over in a broader context, the meaning of the original events has been distorted for various political purposes.

The thesis of this book is that diversity and free expression ought to coexist. And yet, in recent years, on campus after campus, a false choice has been served up: you are either for diversity, equity, and inclusion in our communities or you are for free expression. The strength of our democracy depends on a commitment to upholding both, even—perhaps especially— when it is hardest to do so. The heightened rhetoric of the 2016 presidential campaign, in which the winning candidate took repeated shots at free expression, diversity, equity, and inclusion, only deepened the need to support these values in academic life and beyond—and to establish mechanisms to ensure that these values persist over the long term.

Diversity and free expression ought to coexist not just on our campuses but in increasingly globalized and interconnected societies at large. Debates over free expression in increasingly heterogeneous environments rage from Russia to China and throughout the Middle East and North Africa, as well as in (relatively) liberal democracies such as the United States, the United Kingdom, Canada, and much of continental Europe. States must resolve the same questions as campuses on an ongoing basis: How tolerant can the state be with respect to speech that pushes boundaries? At what point may, or must, the tolerant stop tolerating the intolerant?

In making this argument, I draw on survey research over the past ten years on the topic of free expression, race relations, the freedom to assemble peaceably, and other aspects of the First Amendment. Literature from the fields of diversity and ethnic studies, sociology, education, and the law inform the argument. I draw on my firsthand experience as the Head of School and teacher of U.S. history at Phillips Academy, Andover, a diverse residential high school. I also call on my previous experience as a faculty member and vice-dean at Harvard Law School. The primary audience I have in mind is fellow educators, who must find a good path forward for our communities in a highly charged historical moment.

This topic has urgent, practical ramifications for how we run our campuses and order our societies at large. Tough issues that push and pull on diversity and free speech arise every day, in town squares and on campuses. I will frame the hard, continuously arising questions about where the line between permissible and impermissible speech should be drawn based on our educational goals and values. Every school and university must adopt approaches and policies on these complex topics in every academic year, with ramifications for society at large. And every educational institution should commit itself to teaching our students about the importance of both of these essential concepts and how to grapple with them when they are in tension.

The same challenge that we observe on campuses plays out on the larger scale of states. The rhetoric that propelled Donald Trump to win the presidential election will continue to apply pressure on campuses, as young people learn ways to cope with messages of exclusion of minorities and immigrants, and with attacks on the free expression of individuals and the freedom of the press. When accused of sexual assault, Mr. Trump threatened publicly to sue the women who came forward and the newspapers that covered their allegations. To the extent that President Trump carries out even a subset of the promises he made with respect to exclusion of Muslims, Mexicans, and other non-whites, these issues will remain front and center in the public consciousness. This public awareness will drive campus activity and student activism, and vice versa.

This short book centers on the choices we, as educators, must make in our academic communities. Our policies with respect to free expression and diversity should be grounded in the missions of our institutions. Context matters enormously. Our schools and universities have many things in common; our institutions also have distinct histories, values, and mission statements. The goals that we establish in educational settings—to teach students material they need to know, impart skills they ought to have, and support them in becoming good citizens—should guide how we set our policy and handle controversies as they arise. The institutional setting and the goals we establish for education must be crucial factors in our decision making.

Institutions have valid reasons to react differently to the challenges associated with free expression and diversity, given the different contexts in which they operate and the different educational goals they intend to accomplish. A high school ought to address these issues differently than a college, given the age and the developmental needs of younger students. A state university or a community college may come by its diversity in a very different way than a private school. A private university founded to uphold, for example, Roman Catholic values, might approach these flashpoints differently than a major public research university. A state, given its police power, must consider the chilling effects of rules that ban certain kinds of speech in ways that are different from the school or university context. Rules, culture, and norms in each of these instances can have major consequences for how effective the learning environment is, who feels welcome in each community, and how people relate to one another, on campus or in the community at large. Wherever possible, our educational goals and values should guide our decision making as institutions—and we should find effective ways to teach the importance of these goals and values to our students.

***

In the academic year that began in the fall of 2015 and ended in the spring of 2016, student protests and institutional responses dominated our collective consciousness. Student protests keyed off of national movements aimed at social justice, especially the #BlackLivesMatter movement.[1] The protests led to extensive discussion, often heated, about a host of race-related matters on campuses. The string of high-profile cases involving the death of black males at the hands of police in Ferguson, Missouri; Staten Island, New York; Baltimore, Maryland, and elsewhere brought into public consciousness the higher likelihood for a victim of a police shooting to be a black male than a person of any other demographic. Other leading activists during this period, such as the author and professor Melissa Harris-Perry and the leaders of the #SayHerName campaign, have focused attention on the types of disproportionate harms done to black women.[2]

The essential claims of the student protesters drew on national protests about the importance of black lives—not to the exclusion of other lives, but in addition to the lives of others. Student protests built on these larger claims and extended them to specific issues of campus life: examining the historical and structural racism on campuses, pressing institutions to explore their own pasts in honest ways, and demanding a series of changes to present-day campus life and culture. Students occupied the offices of presidents and other administrators from Princeton to Duke on the East Coast to Occidental on the West Coast. Student demands came together on websites and social media, ricocheting from school to school.[3] High school students held events, rallies, and forums in solidarity with their university counterparts.

University presidents and deans responded in a range of ways. By and large, most academic leaders have taken these student protests seriously and have agreed to meet some, though rarely all, of the student demands. In November 2015, Yale declared it would invest $50 million in an effort to improve faculty diversity over a five-year period. Brown doubled that commitment with a $100 million initiative over ten years to create a more diverse and inclusive community. After a long period of study and community conversations, Harvard Law School announced in 2016 it would discontinue use of a shield that harked back to the crest of the slave-holding family of Isaac Royall, the school's founding donor. Some institutions refused the demands outright. In nearly every instance, the campus activism forced conversations among current administrators, faculty, students, and trustees. These debates also engaged members of the extended alumni bodies of the respective schools in on-campus discussions.

In many cases, the debate strayed from concerns about institutional racism into a debate about free expression. The contours of the conversation varied, but they often took the following form. Protesters expressed their upset over institutional racism or other forms of discrimination. The protesters sought greater support for students of color, increased faculty hiring among underrepresented minorities, cultural competency training for faculty and staff, changes to campus policies, the renaming of buildings, and other diversity-related measures. It was in the process of reacting to these demands that the topic of free expression often arose. This particular connection of diversity and free expression has often been fueled by the national media coverage of campus events. Mainstream news publications, bespoke online blogs, and social media coverage all fanned the flames along the way. Videos captured on smartphones went viral. A hype cycle emerged: it would start with the original dispute, then turn to the campus reaction to the dispute—including statements for and against free expression—and then to the fallout from the reaction, which inevitably drew alumni and families right into the on-campus fray.

On some campuses, those who opposed student demands raised the notion of free expression as they advocated for no change to the status quo. In other cases, opponents accused protesters of stifling free expression when they shouted down those with opposing views; protesters, likewise, claimed that their rights to assemble peaceably and to express themselves had been curtailed. Proponents of guest speakers being barred from campuses, for example at Williams College, claimed that unpopular views could not be expressed in university settings out of an excess of "political correctness." In other cases, faculty members and students claimed that free expression was not as important as the race-related demands—that the free expression rights should be sublimated to a position below the claims related to diversity. In certain cases, free speech provocateurs manipulated campus events in order to create a forum in which to make their case in the public eye. In some instances, campus protesters fell into the trap laid before them by tearing down the posters of those who advocated a different point of view, only to be accused of opposing free expression. In each of these instances, along these varied routes, the principle of improving the diversity, equity, and inclusion of campuses found itself in opposition to the principle of free expression.

***

Free expression and diversity are essential components of democracy in the twenty-first century. In the United States, our shared commitment to both principles, especially as they developed in the late twentieth century, ensures that a democracy and the world at large benefit from heterogeneity. These two concepts rely on and reinforce one another.

The arguments in favor of diversity and free expression are not exactly the same, but neither are they unrelated. There are reasons for diversity that have little or nothing to do with free expression; and there are reasons for free expression that have little or nothing to do with diversity. The areas of overlap, though, are plentiful—and they are essential to finding the best path forward. At their essence, both of these ideals support democracy because they mean that societies are educating informed, engaged citizens and seeking to establish a sense of fair play and justice in political systems. While diversity and free expression are too often pitted against one another as competing values, they are more compatible than they are opposing.

The American experiment at its best calls for diversity and free expression to coexist. That coexistence has not been easy, nor has it been all that successful, especially for those who have had less power. The American experience has been a lot easier for whites, males, Christians, heterosexuals, the able-bodied, and the wealthy in particular. And free expression has been interpreted in ways that have tended to support those in authority rather than all people equitably. These critiques of the American experiment are all grounded in historical truth. But it is also true that free expression can serve all of us. Diversity is about self-expression, learning from one another, working together in productive ways across differences, and in turn strengthening our democracy. Diversity that also encompasses and supports intellectual and academic freedom—without condoning hate speech—has enormous force, promise, and importance.

Our commitment to seeking the truth and making sound decisions, in intellectual communities and in the public sphere, relies on the coexistence of diversity and free expression. One of the reasons to have a diverse community—one in which we truly welcome adults and young people with a broad range of racial, class, ethnic, religious, cultural, and political backgrounds, as well as people with a range of gender and sexual orientations—is that they bring various viewpoints that can help a community reach good, moral, and truthful decisions. This range of viewpoints also helps communities reach just decisions that a broad range of people will believe to be legitimate.

As one example, consider the field of journalism and the need for a diverse corps of reporters to serve a multicultural democracy well. Among other things, a democracy depends on a strong, independent field of journalism to function effectively. Journalism enables the public to stay informed about crucial issues in such a way that the people may determine their own best interests. Journalism offers plentiful examples of this concurrent need for diversity and free expression in support of democracy. A well-trained, professional team of journalists—even if they all come from one racial background, say all Latino/Latina—may be able to cover the stories of a large and complex city with a reasonable degree of accuracy. But getting to the truth of what is really going on in, say, that city's Chinatown section will be enhanced by someone on the staff coming from that neighborhood or from a Chinese-speaking background. At a minimum, that team of reporters would need to rely on sources and informants from Chinatown in order to tell that story with a fidelity to what actually occurred and what it meant. In either event, a diverse set of voices—whether as authors or sources—can lead to a deeper understanding of the truth in a complex environment than a homogeneous group of voices can. In turn, those who rely on this journalism have a greater likelihood of discerning their own true interests and acting accordingly as citizens.[4]

Or consider the discipline of writing and studying U.S. history, which I teach to high school juniors and seniors at Andover. If virtually all the authorities writing prominent history books are men (as they were for a long time), the likelihood is high that their narratives would extol the great male military and political leaders, not the women and many of the people of color who lived then. The idea behind diversifying the ranks of our history teachers and scholars is that a more diverse group of authors will tell a more complete—and correspondingly more truthful—version of what happened. The point is not to eliminate political and military history or the lives of "great men" from our narratives but rather to include social and cultural history—for instance, as it is told by women or people of color, unwelcome in political and military leadership for much of our history. The point is also not that only African Americans can write about the lives of those enslaved or what it was like to be subject to Jim Crow laws, but rather that having a more diverse group of teachers and authors results in a broader range of perspectives. As the professoriate continues to become more diverse, the narratives that we teach in history are becoming more diverse and richer.

Free expression, likewise, enables us to find the truth. If certain views are unwelcome or barred, then the likelihood that societies will find or embrace the truth diminishes. The extreme case is an authoritarian regime for instance, in North Korea—where dissent is nearly impossible and the free flow of ideas is nonexistent. If criticism of political figures, whether accurate or not, is disallowed or strongly discouraged—as it is, for instance, in present-day Turkey, Russia, or Thailand—then the likelihood that the truth about their activities will emerge is much lower. When Saddam Hussein received 100 percent of the votes cast in the election of 2002—all 11,445,638 of them—one can reasonably infer that the Iraqi people were not free to discuss the potential shortcomings of the next Hussein administration.[5] In the case of the urban journalists, free expression supports understanding of the real dynamics at play in Chinatown. In the case of the historians, free expression enables broader consideration of events and patterns that had previously lain uncovered—and that may have been inconvenient to unearth, discuss, and publish. Without commitment to free expression, the truth is much less likely to emerge. Without a route to the truth, the likelihood of good policy decisions, fair dealing with communities, and just outcomes of disputes is much lower.

Diversity and free expression are linked, too, as principles that lead to higher levels of equity and fairness. The success of these ideals provides legitimacy for a democratic system. One reason to pursue a diverse environment, especially in a school or university setting, is to ensure that every young person has a roughly equal chance at the positive gains possible through education. If a school admits only young people of a single race, gender, ethnicity, faith, sexuality, or type of ability, then the opportunities at that school are not equitably afforded to those with other characteristics. In a knowledge-dominated economy, access to the benefits of education is of fundamental importance. Diversity initiatives—including but not limited to affirmative action policies—aim to ensure that the inequities of the past are not paid for in the future. These commitments ensure that every member of an academic environment feels and is valued for what they offer to the community and can accomplish while in school and afterward. The benefits of addressing inequity on campus connect directly to the degree of equality in the polity at large.

Free expression, in its purest form, is also a driver of equity and justice. Free expression means that no voice is categorically entitled to greater freedom than any other. At the level of principle, freedom of expression is even-handed: it means that the color of one's skin, or faith, or sexuality should not be a bar to expressing one's point of view, participating in civic life through speech, and so forth. In practice, in most societies, this form of equity has rarely existed: some people are able to speak louder and more freely than others.

Free expression is linked to a series of other freedoms with similar connections to equity. In the context of the United States, these freedoms are enshrined in the First Amendment to the Constitution: the right to free speech and a free press, the right to assemble peaceably, and the right to religious beliefs. Alongside the right to free expression, these other rights also protect those who might otherwise suffer persecution: the unpopular minority group has the right to come together peaceably in a community, or to pursue their faith, or to publish their views through a specialized press, or to seek redress from the government. Taken together, these rights have great force on behalf of an equitable society.

***

The matter, of course, is not as simple as saying that diversity and free expression are mutually supportive concepts, on campus and in society at large. There are serious theoretical arguments to the contrary. There are hard cases that make these principles difficult to reconcile. The hardest cases, customarily involving hate speech, require balancing of competing interests that can leave no one happy.

The most forceful argument, expressed from the political left, against my view that these two principles should coexist comes with the (truthful) claim that the right to free expression arose in the context of inequality. The First Amendment to the U.S. Constitution, for instance, was drafted by white, powerful men of European descent—many of whom enslaved their fellow Americans. Moreover, the interpretation of the right of free expression in the United States has been historically carried out by and large by male judges, often white and well off. Given this history, the right to free expression has been a tool of empowered people, not those who have been marginalized. As such, this counterargument goes, the right to free expression is flawed and less worthy of support than diversity, equity, and inclusion, especially where these two values conflict. While I acknowledge the force of this argument, I think it is less compelling than the claim that the two principles, in a more equitable historical moment, can and should be upheld in common.

Other counterarguments take issue with either the specific application of free expression or diversity or both. It is one thing to make a broad claim about the importance of diversity and free expression coexisting; it is quite another to determine how best to apply them in an actual society.

Free expression, for instance, evokes a range of possible policies, from one in which truly "anything goes" to the constrained version of free expression (which I favor) that is enshrined in the U.S. Constitution. This latter vision of free expression calls for limits to free expression in certain circumstances, known as "time, place, and manner" restrictions. Gender and racial harassment, fighting words, obscenity, and libel, for instance, are not protected speech even under the First Amendment. In the context of a campus, the limits to free expression often take another form: disallowing students from using hate speech targeted at another student, for instance. None of these types of restrictions on free expression would bar citizens or students from expressing a political opinion, however unpopular, as long as it does not target or put at risk another person. While some disagree with the idea of any restrictions on free expression, others wish for speech restrictions to further limit or ban certain additional forms of speech.

A similar counterargument might take issue with the forms of diversity that I favor in this book. As in the case of free expression, the views fall along a broad spectrum. On the one end, diversity extends to a strong form of equality and inclusion, brought about by affirmative policies intended to accomplish what proponents refer to as "social justice." On the other end of the spectrum falls extreme xenophobia—whether expressed by white supremacists or by those who express hatred toward others from a religious viewpoint. For the purposes of this argument, I favor a form of diversity that makes good on the promises of the American ideal: a nation that invites those from all over the world to form a community together, representing a range of backgrounds and viewpoints. On campuses, this ideal means seeking young people from all over the country and the world, from all races, ethnicities, faith backgrounds, sexual orientations, with a range of abilities, and from families with different political viewpoints. Here, too, there are, and must be, restrictions of various sorts. A nation must limit those who can immigrate in certain ways in order to avoid systems being overwhelmed by the sheer number of residents; similarly, enrollment on a campus ought to be limited to a number of students who can in fact thrive in that particular learning environment. Some might agree that this definition of diversity is too generous; others might oppose the limits I suggest or favor more radical policies to accomplish the goals of diversity, equity, and inclusion.

The hardest theoretical problem in holding these two ideals together is not one of definition, as thorny as that can be—it has to do with a paradox at the heart of this combination. One goal of diversity, equity, and inclusion—taken together—is tolerance. These ideals call for a community to enable all members to enjoy equal privileges. This notion of equity is especially hard to accomplish in environments that have been the least equal in the past—for instance, campuses that have only recently been opened to those of a certain gender or race, where intolerance has been the norm for a long time. The paradox becomes evident when someone does not believe in tolerance. The belief they hold—or the expression they wish to convey freely—is that the very idea of tolerance is wrong.

Must a community tolerate intolerance? It is this hard problem that presented itself on so many campuses in the fall of 2015 and again in the presidential election of 2016, and that will remain with us for the foreseeable future. Some campus activists argue for no as an answer to that question. From my perspective, the answer is yes, at least to some extent. Tolerance must extend not only to those who believe in tolerance but also to those who do not. In a democratic system at large, we give votes regardless of a person's viewpoint. As humans and communities, we learn when we are presented with viewpoints different from our own.

The difficulty with this idea—and the primary shortcoming of the view that we must tolerate some degree of intolerant speech—is that the costs of such tolerance will be borne disproportionately by those who are the targets of the intolerance. In America, those people are likely the same people whose forebears have been the targets of intolerance in the past: people of color, women, those who identify as LGBTQIA+, those who do not identify squarely on the cis-gendered binary (female or male), and those with different abilities. This argument—that we ought to hold diversity and free expression as mutually reinforcing principles—is at its most vulnerable when we consider the disproportionality of the costs of extreme tolerance.

There are ways to mitigate this problem, though it may be a long time (or a rare place) before the problem is fully addressed. The roots of discrimination are long and run deep; they are not easily pulled out of any soil, without trace or likelihood of regrowth.

One form of mitigation is to limit free expression in specific ways. There must be a point at which the tolerant should not have to tolerate the intolerant. One limitation, sensibly included in campus policies, is to disallow hate speech personally directed at an individual. If a member of the community directs hate speech at another individual (rather than at a group), the speech can be subject to restriction and the speaker to disciplinary measures or other recourse. Specific campuses or communities might have narrowly tailored rules along these lines to protect those most vulnerable. It is easy to imagine that rules at a school for young children would be even more protective in this respect than the rules at a high school or those at a university, given the different educational aims of these types of institutions and different maturity levels of their students.

Where a speaker expresses a general political viewpoint, communities must seek to tolerate these expressions, even if she or he preaches something inconsistent with the majority viewpoint on campus. If this political speech is intolerant toward some community members, the response should be to address this intolerant viewpoint with more speech. An affirmative obligation to speak up falls on those who oppose the position. In a civic context, it is imperative that citizens and political leaders speak up to defend the rights of all people in the community. This burden must not fall just on those threatened by the speech; those who already feel the most marginalized, undervalued, or invisible in communities may find it hard to voice their concerns. The burden ought to fall less on those directly affected and more on those who are in the favored position. In the campus context, those representing the institution itself—a college president, a university board chair, or a school principal—ought to establish a point of view that favors tolerance, diversity, equity, and inclusion over hate and intolerance. The best approach for the long run is for the truthful, positive, values-driven viewpoint to be given the chance to win out. The stronger argument should prove more sustainable and more broadly embraced over time if it is contested than if it is merely insisted on without interrogation. To impose a rule against the less tolerant political viewpoint, or to ban that viewpoint from the commons, would have high costs in the long run, but so too does tolerating certain hateful speech on campuses.

In this book, I advance an argument that goes one step further. To the extent that an educational community's mission is to promote diversity, equity, and inclusion as well as free expression, I believe that sharper limits—including limits that might not be allowed under today's First Amendment jurisprudence—can be appropriate, as long as these limits are disclosed to students in advance. Just as I argue that obnoxious political speech must be tolerated to a degree, I argue that there should be a limit to the types and ways in which hateful speech may be uttered. The mission of the educational institution must guide the school's practices in this respect. There is a point at which the educational values of creating a supportive, equitable learning environment are more powerful than the importance of supporting unfettered speech, even when one might do so in the public square. There is a point at which intolerance of the intolerant is not only acceptable but appropriate in a learning community. To find that place in our schools and universities can be a great challenge, but we need systems that enable us to find it. We also need educational systems that teach students ways to engage in debates about free expression and diversity, which they will inevitably face when the leave the shelter of schools and universities.

***

The debates that raged on campuses in 2014, 2015, and 2016 have ramifications far beyond the walls of any individual school. These debates press us to articulate the purpose of education and the values we espouse as schools. The theoretical implications of these debates also matter to the way societies operate. Campuses are, to a degree, microcosms of increasingly diverse, interconnected communities and societies. When students leave our campuses, they go on to populate and to lead our states, nations, regions, and global communities.

Rapid changes to the manner in which people use technology make this problem thornier. Localized events on campuses today can become public, global events very quickly. The ubiquity of social media, recording devices on nearly every phone, and a political environment in which these topics have important currency have changed the nature of the campus dialogue. Campus protests of the past, too, have had the capacity to create national news—think of the Kent State protests against the Cambodia invasion and subsequent shootings in 1970. Today, far less dramatic encounters can become major news stories, with first-person accounts recorded and published instantaneously to Twitter, Facebook, or YouTube. The rules that relate to technology and speech—particularly in authoritarian regimes—connect directly to this debate as well. To the extent that we fail to build diverse communities capable of tolerating a broad range of speech, it is more likely that regimes will favor xenophobia and restrictions on the open Internet—a technological system that can support the free exchange of ideas and support diverse communities, but that can also be manipulated to accomplish quite the opposite.

Events on campuses directly connect to the town square, to national forums, and to the interconnected global commons. This interconnection is plainly a good thing: our campuses ought to be connected to the world from which students and faculty come and to which they will go. As any teacher knows, a student who feels connected to the subject matter in a larger sense is more likely to be engaged in learning than a student who considers the topic irrelevant. It is essential that these principles can coexist on campuses so that they can coexist in the communities beyond. It is also essential that the young people we are educating today become able to coexist with others in the increasingly heterogeneous environments in which they will live as adults. Much turns on the outcome.

As educators, we ought to create for our students both safe spaces and brave spaces in which they can learn and thrive. By safe spaces, I do not refer to the types of rooms dominated by soft cushions and plush toys that have been decried in the media. Safe spaces are environments in which students can explore ideas and express themselves in a context with well-understood ground rules for the conversation. For instance, a school or university might create a safe space for LGBTQ students in which students know they can discuss issues of sexual identity or gender and will not be made to feel marginalized for their perspective or exploration. The University of Chicago's

Office of LGBTQ Student Life has a Safe Space program that provides such an environment.[6] A safe space might be moderated by an adult or peer skilled in understanding particular topics related to the development of the young people seeking that particular environment. A safe space might be a literal room in a building or it might be a periodic session that moves from place to place. The rules and norms that govern the conversation might well be more restrictive than the rules and norms set forth in the First Amendment. Ideally, these safe spaces would also be environments in which students would find support, develop coping skills, and hone effective techniques for communicating with one another in a way that honors tolerance, avoids stereotypes, and cuts down on hate on campuses.

By brave spaces, I refer to learning environments that approximate the world outside academic life. Brave spaces include classrooms, lecture halls, and public forums where the rules and social norms for expression might in fact follow the doctrine of the First Amendment or something close to it, as set by the school or university at large. Brave spaces are those learning environments in which the primary purpose of the interaction is a search for the truth, rather than support for a particular group of students, even insofar as some of the discussions will be uncomfortable for certain students. I would imagine that for students at most institutions, time spent in brave spaces would make up the vast majority of their time during their education. Some spaces might also serve as a blend of the two ideas, with well-articulated expectations set out by the teacher or discussion leader at the outset. The balance between brave spaces and safe spaces would hinge on the specific goals and values of each institution.[7]

The creation of both brave spaces and safe spaces entails creating environments in which students are at once challenged and supported in their learning. It also calls on us to ground our approach to disputes over free expression and diversity in our institution's core values—and to communicate that connection with force and clarity through our teaching and our public statements. The policies that we establish in campus communities must be tied to our educational goals. These policies must be clear and understandable to faculty, staff, and students. Our decisions based on these policies are consequential. So, too, are the practices that we favor on campuses. In setting these policies and carrying out these practices, we should resist pitting diversity against free expression. Rather, we should seek to find where they intersect to the fullest degree. We need both of these values to flourish in order to have strong schools, producing good citizens who will go on to live in and lead thriving democracies.

2 Flashpoints

The 2016 academic year began with a bang when the University of Chicago's dean of students, John Ellison, issued a letter to incoming undergraduate students about what they might expect on campus. In his letter, Dean Ellison wrote: "Our commitment to academic freedom means that we do not support so-called 'trigger warnings,' we do not cancel invited speakers because their topics might prove controversial and we do not condone the creation of intellectual 'safe spaces' where individuals can retreat from ideas and perspectives at odds with their own."[1] Dean Ellison's letter came against the backdrop of rising student activism around the country and the University of Chicago's strong, historic stance on freedom of expression.

Dean Ellison's opening-of-school letter reignited the raging debate on campuses, in the mainstream media, and online over free expression and student activism. Those who have railed against political correctness and a restricted campus environment for speech cheered the clarity of the University of Chicago dean's statement.[2] Other observers pointed out that Ellison's letter belittled the student concerns that had given rise to their protests over the past few academic years. Some noted that the dean's letter seemed aimed more at the university's donors than at its incoming students.[3] Still others thought that Dean Ellison's clarion call missed the mark in dismissing legitimate campus practices that support increasingly diverse populations.

The letter was certainly effective at one thing: people read it, not just on campus but all over the world. Most of these letters are dreadful to write and even worse to read. In 2016, the customarily boring opening-of-school letters and speeches to incoming students became important, much-watched statements of perspective from academic administrators. The controversy surrounding the Chicago letter brought to a head many of the debates that had been raging on campuses for years. It served as a powerful prompt for every school and university to work through issues related to campus climate and other important public concerns on the minds of the students.[4]

College presidents and administrators face a wide array of challenges in any given year. The job of keeping a school afloat is hard enough: hiring and retaining a great faculty, recruiting and educating a diverse student body, connecting with alumni and fundraising from them, maintaining a physical campus and its virtual counterparts, and so forth. Add in the task of responding to student activism and the job, on certain days anyway, can feel overwhelming. The same is true for deans, principals, and heads of schools. No administrator can keep every constituency happy all the time; public statements that say anything of substance are certain to displease someone, especially on the hot-button issues at the heart of student activism. Students are the reason for schools and colleges to exist; at the same time, through their activism they certainly confront administrators with hard problems.

The academic years from 2014 to 2017 have been dramatic from the perspective of campus activism. This uptick in student activism is not unprecedented in U.S. history; however, one of the fascinating subtexts is the extent to which many current academic administrators were themselves involved in campus activism in the 1960s and 1970s. Those who protested against Vietnam, racial injustice, and a myriad of other problems a generation ago are now working in the very same campus administrative offices they once occupied in a very different posture: as protesters.

The range of student concerns voiced in the past few years has been broad. Popular causes have included divestment from the assets of businesses that particularly affect climate change; policies and practices related to rape culture and sexual assault; the pernicious effects of high-stakes academic testing; the rising cost of higher education; and so forth.[5] The types and duration of activities on campuses have varied, but anyone working in academia during this period would report that student activism has played an important role in the life of our educational institutions.

By far the most prominent set of drivers of campus activism has centered on racial inequities and social justice more broadly. This strain of activism has been intense, sustained, and connected across campuses and beyond. The concerns raised by students have focused both on conditions in schools and in the world at large. Extrajudicial killings of black males by police have served as the proximate cause of many demonstrations. The underlying issue has been the systemic racism extending from the communities where the killings occurred to the campuses themselves. The issues raised by students have united the communities across the United States in which they grew up and the campuses they now call their (academic) homes. The concerns they have raised speak directly to the experiences of young people of color, as well as adults of color, on campuses that have historically been predominantly white. Student activism has also exposed other forms of difference based on gender, sexuality, faith, economic class, disability, and so forth.

Race-centered student activism has led to many significant changes in higher education. In the fall of 2015, the president and chancellor of the University of Missouri resigned from their posts in the wake of demonstrations caused by their handling of racially charged events on campus.[6] Yale, Brown, and other universities have committed tens of millions of dollars in new funds to address diversity issues on campus.[7] Many other campuses have pressed forward with equity and inclusion initiatives that previously languished. Students have not achieved all the goals they have set forth in their demands, but their activism has led to significant changes at many institutions.

The students have a point. Institutions are right to listen and to take these concerns seriously. There are, as ever, excesses. Sometimes students overplay their hand; in other cases, students treat shabbily adults who are thoughtful, supportive, and engaged in their work—including scholars who have spent their entire careers working for social justice. Institutions cannot and should not accede to all of their demands. But the fact that students make frivolous demands does not mean that all of their demands lack merit. Those of us who work on these campuses will be well served to think hard about what these young people are saying. They are demanding our attention and we ought to respond in kind with seriousness of purpose. The activism itself, while challenging, ultimately serves a learning purpose. The substance of the student claims deserves a meaningful response, even when the answer is no, as it must be in certain cases.

The campus activism has drawn attention to how unprepared many of us are to talk openly and seriously about race and other social issues, and to reach out to one another across our differences. The empathy that we extend to students ought to also extend to the adults. Many of them—including teachers and administrators living and working on campuses—have not developed the skills and the language of diversity, equity, and inclusion. This language is not mere pablum—it carries a deep meaning to the many students steeped in it and it is essential for educators to grapple with it, too. For those educators (I am among them) who have grown up white, heterosexual, in the middle or upper-middle class (and with any number of other traditional advantages), it can be hard to understand the experiences of those who have grown up with fewer such advantages. Many of the most prominent educational institutions have been dominated by white leaders and students for their entire histories. A big part of this campus activism has been a wake-up call to expand our language and skills in empathy and inclusion, both at the institutional and personal level.

This activism has also given rise to heated conversations about the way our campuses should operate. At many schools and universities, students, faculty, administrators, and alumni have argued about the fundamental values of our educational institutions. Too often, those arguments have involved pitting greater degrees of equity and inclusion against a robust environment for free expression. These debates have often centered on specific flashpoints: safe spaces, trigger warnings, microaggressions, calls to disinvite speakers on campus, and proposals to change symbols or naming decisions on campuses (see figure 2.1).[8] To take each of these topics seriously, and to attend to them as practices

Rules and norms governing the learning environment	Names and symbols that convey institutional values	Types of support and training for community members	Determination of who is included, who has power and voice
Examples: • Speech codes (e.g., 1980s, 1990s, today) • Hazing, harassment, and bullying (statutes, policies, and procedures) • Norms and rules with respect to microaggressions • Norms and rules with respect to trigger warnings	**Examples:** • School names (e.g., Woodrow Wilson at Princeton) • Building names (e.g., Calhoun College at Yale) • Statues (e.g., Cecil Rhodes at Oriel College, Oxford) • Shields (e.g., Royall Family Crest at Harvard Law School	**Examples:** • Programming (for adults, for students; voluntary, mandatory) • Training (for adults, for students; voluntary, mandatory) • Dedicated spaces for marginalized groups (e.g., safe space for LGBTQ community at University of Chicago)	**Examples:** • Recruiting procedures • Admissions process (including affirmative action policies) • Hiring and promotion procedures • Administrative hires • Retention practices • Invitations to speak on campus (on ordinary days, at commencement)

Figure 2.1
Typology of debates over freedom of expression and diversity in academic settings

in a campus environment, does not mean turning one's back on a commitment to a strong form of free expression.

***

The concept of safe spaces on campuses often comes up first. Some believe safe spaces to be essential elements of campus life; others believe them to be a sign of "coddling" our twenty-first-century students.[9] Just as our student bodies and faculties are increasingly diverse, so too should be our campuses. As educators, we should provide students with *safe* spaces and *brave* spaces in which to live and learn. Both are important to human development and flourishing, especially during students' high school and university experiences.

Most campuses do, in fact, provide a combination of safe spaces and brave spaces for students. Most people benefit from some sort of safe space in their life. That might be as simple as the kitchen or "hearth" at home to which we retreat after a busy day, surrounded by family or friends. This safe space is an environment in which one can "be oneself" in a manner different from the public-facing persona one assumes during the rest of the day.

Campuses should ensure that students have this sort of safe space in their lives. At residential schools, that safe space might be a dorm room or a dorm common space. It might be an affinity group for students of a particular background, race, gender, ethnicity, sexuality, or faith. Students of Jewish background might congregate at a university's local Hillel, for instance.[10] It might be the locker room of a sports team that a student plays on or the café adjacent to the theater or music building. The specific nature of these spaces matters less than their purpose: these are environments that allow for students to express themselves in a manner that feels materially different—safer—than in the classroom or in the town square. These spaces are often run by adults or peers who are well trained in facilitation and support for students in certain marginalized groups. Students need these environments to decompress and to explore ideas without fear or a sensation of risk.

One of the ironies of the opening letter from the University of Chicago's dean is that Chicago itself offers environments that they call "safe spaces," in fact explicitly. To make matters more complex, the dean who wrote the letter decrying safe spaces is himself listed on a public university website as a member of the "Safe Space Ally Network" for LGBTQ students.[11] For all the apparent clarity and bluster of his letter, the dean appeared to be a supporter of safe spaces—appropriately—in certain circumstances. (In subsequent statements, the University of Chicago has told representatives of FIRE, the Foundation for Individual Rights in Education, that despite the language of the letter, the university has not issued an outright ban on space spaces and the use of trigger warnings.)[12]

Campuses must also create brave spaces for students, in addition to these safe spaces. The classroom is an obvious example; so, too, might be an amphitheater or a public quadrangle. Ideally, these brave spaces are environments where students are encouraged to engage in serious, respectful, and empathetic discourse as part of their education. Campuses at large need to remain places where students learn to confront the uncomfortable and the unfamiliar and respond in ways that enable them to grow.

This distinction between safe and brave spaces has the added benefit of revealing the way the First Amendment works. An essential step in determining whether a speech act is protected is to evaluate the forum in which the speech occurred. The type of forum helps to guide the level of restriction of speech that a court will deem permissible. For instance, a traditional public forum—such as a public park, or "Speaker's Corner" in London's Hyde Park—is customarily afforded the highest level of speech protection. Campuses often have designated public forums as places set aside for public interaction. Nonpublic forums, such as a room in a dormitory or in an administrative building, might be subject to greater degrees of restriction, consistent with the purpose set forth for that location.

This distinction between the rules appropriate for certain forums and contexts plays out every day. Consider a heckler who stands in a public park near a street corner, waiting for a candidate for a public office to walk by. When the candidate passes in front of him, the heckler shouts a series of epithets at her or him. The police would be hard-pressed to arrest the heckler, unless his speech were truly extreme—provoking imminent harm to the candidate, for instance. If that same heckler were to stand up in the middle of a televised debate between the candidate and a rival and say the same things, the heckler could be removed by security guards for disturbing the proceedings. Various factors come into play in this example: the police and security guards represent different bodies and invoke different kinds of force. The police are agents of the public, while the security guards are privately hired. At its essence, this example demonstrates that the forum and context matter a great deal in the extent to which a speech might be regulated.

An incident reported on the campus of DePaul University, not far from the University of Chicago, put the topic of safe spaces in yet another light. According to news reports, a hotly debated speaking event drew a mix of DePaul students and outsiders to the campus. Some of the people attending the event popped their head into a campus multicultural center to taunt those inside: "Is this your safe space?"[13] The cruelty of this reported act sets in context the debate over safe spaces: Is it really too much for campuses to provide gathering spaces where young people can learn without being mocked for their identity, if they desire to congregate with others from a similar background for part of a day?

To support safe spaces is in no way to turn one's back on brave spaces in academic communities. Many college presidents and deans issued opening statements in the fall of 2016, calling on students to engage in uncomfortable conversations and to face hard ideas and topics. We must aim to get our students to stretch, just as great schools have always done, and we should also support them wholeheartedly. The only thing that has changed with time is that we now realize that we ought to be more broad-minded about the nature of the support we provide and the range of safe—and brave—spaces we make available to students on our campuses, especially as they grow more diverse.

***

A second flashpoint: trigger warnings. Imagine a course in the literature department in which students are about to read a novel. The book contains an especially graphic and potentially upsetting scene of rape. The teacher who is about to teach the course is aware that sexual assault on campus has continued to be an area of concern, after a quarter or more of the undergraduates have reported experiencing assault. Several student protests during the previous term have drawn attention to the notion that a "rape culture" pervades the community and must be addressed. Before the students begin the reading assignment, the teacher mentions that the book may have a "triggering" effect for those who have been affected by sexual assault, either directly or indirectly. On the same campus, when a violent film is about to be shown, an administrator might issue a similar warning at the outset of the event, informing students of the film's potential triggering effect.

The concept of trigger warnings has prompted critics to say that our schools are "coddling" students and promoting self-censorship. Trigger warnings, the critique goes, represent a trend in which schools stay away from assigning challenging texts and thus "dumb down" their curricula. Faculty members refrain from assigning certain texts, the concern goes, for fear that they will lead to student protests or complaints.

The critics of trigger warnings have several points in their favor. Trigger warnings could be taken too far; it is easy to make them seem ridiculous. For a school or university to mandate trigger warnings before students are exposed to any text, speaker, movie, play, or other public event would be a mistake. Such a rule would be extraordinarily hard to interpret and enforce. Since part of the job of schools and universities is to prepare students for the world outside academia, it would be a terrible mistake—and an extension of a nefarious trend in parenting—to create a false environment in which students never experience or endure discomfort of any kind. Trigger warnings, mandated and carried out to an extreme, would be counterproductive to some of the most essential goals of education.

That does not mean that trigger warnings are inherently bad. Trigger warnings, used sensibly in moderation by caring people, are simply good teaching. Put another way, borrowing the language of *The Economist*, trigger warnings are "good manners."[14] A school or university that supports its teachers and administrators in using trigger warnings where, in their judgment, they are advisable hardly involves censorship of the material that might be offensive to students. To the contrary, trigger warnings may make students better prepared to handle exactly the kinds of challenging ideas that critics are concerned are being banished from intellectual life on campus. Yes, a trigger warning might cause a student to opt out of a certain public event, for instance, but that student has always been free to skip a lecture and perhaps find another way to engage with the material in another context.

There might be at least three possible policies on trigger warnings. One policy might ban trigger warnings—the approach that the University of Chicago dean of students seemed to call for in his 2016 opening address. A second policy might mandate trigger warnings. A third policy might support teachers and administrators, as well as student organizers, in using trigger warnings when their judgment calls for it. From the perspective of academic freedom, the first two policies (the ban or the mandate) are the least satisfactory. The right approach is the third policy, one wholly consistent with principles both of free expression and academic freedom. To the extent that one supports the autonomy of teachers in the classroom, one must permit trigger warnings by teachers, or whatever the teacher decides to call them.

***

A third flashpoint: microaggressions. One effect of the increased diversity in academic environments is that some people experience inequities more directly and consistently than others do. This problem is not exclusive to the academy; it is part and parcel of the world we live in. In the United States, it is more likely, overall, that an African-American customer in a high-end retail outlet will be followed around by a store employee than a white customer will. An African American is much more likely to be stopped for a traffic violation or put in jail for a drug offense. These differences are empirically proven over and over again.[15]

Student activism has focused in recent years on the experiences of those who feel—and often are—marginalized on campuses. Student leaders, with support and backing from adults, have pointed to many areas where schools and universities still have a long way to go to be equitable and inclusive. Many elite institutions, especially in the United States, are still predominantly white in terms of visible leadership, faculty, and student composition. The *Chronicle of Higher Education* has shown that 33 percent of first-year students at four-year institutions in the United States identified as people of color (Asian, black, and Latino/a, combined) as of 2014.[16] That same survey showed that about 20 percent of faculty members self-identified in these same categories.[17] In 2013, the National Center for Educational Statistics showed that 16 percent of full-time college professors identified as people of color and 84 percent as white.[18] This representation of people of color in higher education remains sharply lower overall than in U.S. society as a whole. While demographics and other factors are changing quickly in certain places, the fact remains: many students and adults of color feel less welcome and less central to life in their academic communities.

The experience of feeling marginalized is not exclusively linked to race and ethnicity. A whole slew of factors can lead to these experiences—differences in social and economic class, gender, sexuality, faith, types of ability, age, and political viewpoints can make students feel marginalized on campus. The experience of marginalization is context specific and often overlooked, but it is very real in any community that is meaningfully diverse.

This experience of inequity is tied to the fact that at many schools and universities, at a macro-level, students from underrepresented minorities, despite similar aptitude, can find it harder to attain grades as high as the grades achieved by students in other demographic groups. As legal scholar Lani Guinier has shown, even when these students come in with roughly equivalent test scores and previous grades, they often do less well academically than their counterparts from other groups. Guinier's work prompts us to ask the important question of why this particular form of inequity should persist in our elite educational institutions.[19]

The dynamic of intersectionality leads to some of these inequities. Intersectionality is the notion that forms of difference can be compounded for people in a community—that they intersect in ways that increase the effects of prejudice felt by the adult or student. The students and adults who experience the highest degree of marginalization in an academic community are often those whose backgrounds have placed them in the community's minority in more than one respect. In other words, the experience of a heterosexual, Asian male might be quite different from the experience of a bisexual, Asian woman, and so forth. This intersectionality creates a kaleidoscopically complex picture in terms of the range and confluence of possible experiences on campus.

Against this complex backdrop, the discussion of microaggressions comes into relief. In the course of daily life on campus, some people experience more slights—both intended and unintended—than other people do, and for a range of reasons. Over the past forty years or so, several academics have developed theories trying to explain microaggressions: Harvard's Chester M. Pierce, MIT's Mary Rowe (who also used the term *microinequities*), and Columbia's Derald Wing Sue.[20] Other scholars, including Stanford's Claude Steele, have linked the notion of microaggressions to the notion of stereotype threats.[21]

Let's stipulate for a moment that the issue of microaggressions is real. (Not everyone agrees; some will surely read these words with dismay or trepidation.)

The first frame of reference is to acknowledge that there is a difference between intent and impact. One of the critiques of the term *microaggression* is that it implies that the person uttering the slight or carrying out the insensitive action is intending to be "aggressive." The intent/impact distinction helps resolve this tension. It is entirely possible, and in fact often true, that a speaker means one thing and the listener hears something quite different. That divide may be the result of power dynamics, cultural differences, an absence of additional cues (especially in the context of digital media), or other factors. This distinction neither undercuts the fact that the person speaking may have no intention of causing harm, nor does it dismiss the experience of the listener of feeling slighted.

A second frame of reference is a culture that encourages addressing the existence of microaggressions without fear of reprisal. Microaggressions make many people worry as— regardless of race or background—we are all liable to carry out microaggressions by accident. No one could possibly predict all the ways one's words or actions might slight another person. The concept of implicit bias means that everyone holds biases that we do not fully understand ourselves. Every culture and community has its own distinct history. This means that we all might end up acting insensitively to culturally different others. As our communities grow more diverse, the probability of micro-aggressions grows as well.

In setting policies, schools and universities must draw their own lines between issues that can be handled informally— through a one-on-one or mediated conversation—and matters that have to be treated more formally. A common strategy is to establish a mechanism for bringing up a case of microaggres-sion to an adult trained professionally to resolve issues of equity and inclusion. That adult can help to calibrate the appropriate level of concern and help the person affected seek proportionate redress within the campus community. The most harmful cases are commonly referred to administrators or faculty who assess hazing, harassment, and bullying, often under the mandate of a state law.

It would be a mistake for every microaggression to lead to a sanction or to a formal institutional response of any kind. To do so would slow the gears of a community to a near-halt, given how frequently microaggressions occur. To do so would also establish a culture in which students would be hard-pressed to learn how to cope with the inevitable slights that await us all outside the doors of the academy. In addition, aggressive institutional responses to microaggressions could lead to the chilling of speech. It is possible to accept that microaggressions matter, without committing to turning each one into a disciplinary case. It is reasonable, too, to acknowledge that microaggressions occur disproportionately to some members of our communities; that because of intersectionality some people may experience a compounded effect of microaggressions; and that campus leaders have an obligation to take them seriously when they get in the way of the business of teaching and learning. Ideally, the way schools handle microaggressions would give rise to new opportunities for teaching and learning the important skill of cultural and intercultural competency.

***

A fourth flashpoint: disinviting speakers. In the past several years, the list of speakers disinvited from giving speeches on campuses has grown long. The invitation to Condoleezza Rice, for instance, to speak at Rutgers University led to a petition to disinvite her for her role in the decision making that led up to the second Iraq War. An invitation to Christine Lagarde, the first woman to run the International Monetary Fund, to speak at Smith College led to a petition to disinvite her because, the critics said, the IMF stood for capitalist values antithetical to those of the college community.[22]

Those who oppose campus speakers, of course, have a right to express their contrary opinions. Administrators and trustees need to devote real care to inviting speakers who will meaningfully add to campus discourse. And choosing commencement speakers deserves special care, given that the ceremony has great significance for graduates and that "avoiding" the speech is more difficult than avoiding a voluntary lecture or program offered in the middle of a term. Moreover, the venue for a speech, the way the institution introduces the speaker, and the age of the students enrolled all make a big difference.

Insisting on disinviting speakers because of their political views, particularly at major universities, runs counter to the basic principles of academic freedom and rigorous intellectual discourse. These "disinvitation" calls undercut the legitimate concerns about the importance of viewpoint diversity and of efforts to make our campuses truly inclusive, equitable, and ethical. There are better ways to counter speech that might be antithetical to the viewpoints of students on campus without violating the principle of academic freedom. Hold signs outside the event. Hold a press conference about how outrageous the speaker's position is. Host a competing event, or two or three. Write op-eds. Advocate zealously. Campus activists—who so often have an important point to make about how we run our academic institutions—lose credibility when they call for banning controversial guest speakers, especially those whose words can be easily avoided.

***

A fifth flashpoint: the renaming of prominent campus spaces and symbols. Rather than obscure with hyperbole what is really going on in these campus disputes, we should focus on how to teach, challenge, and engage our students in a robust debate, while respecting that students have a point about the climate on our campuses and the history of our institutions. The climate on campus can and does feel different to students, depending on where they come from and how they are treated in our communities. Conflicts are highly likely, perhaps inevitable, on our campuses, especially as we (rightly) strive to make them more diverse along many dimensions.

As an example of a positive way to honor these twin principles while engaging students and adults in debate, consider the way that Harvard Law School Dean Martha Minow addressed concerns about the school's shield in 2016. In 1936, the Harvard Corporation adopted for the law school a shield based on the family crest of an eighteenth-century slaveholder, Isaac Royall, who had given funds to support the first chair in law at Harvard.[23] Dean Minow asked a veteran law professor, Bruce Mann, to lead a group of faculty and students to consider whether the shield continued to make sense as the school's symbol at this moment in history. The committee conferred with more than 1,000 people. After public forums and thoughtful consideration, Dean Minow and the Harvard Corporation in 2016 accepted the committee's recommendation in support of a change in the image on the shield.[24] The Harvard Corporation may or may not decide on a new shield in the coming years as Harvard Law School prepares to celebrate its 200th anniversary year. Online exhibits and materials about the school's history have been mounted to promote continued discourse. At least one professor on the committee, the historian and law professor Annette Gordon-Reed, and one student, Annie Rittgers, disagreed in a public statement released along with the school's decision.[25] This serious and respectful exchange of ideas has led to a greater understanding of the school's history and its values—and will continue to do so over the next few years.

Harvard Law School has had plenty of company when it comes to calls to change a school's symbol or reconsider an old naming decision. Faced with similar questions, Yale University has adopted a thoughtful policy for how to consider historical symbols on campus, such as the name of one of its residential colleges, which honors former U.S. Vice President John C. Calhoun, one of history's most outspoken supporters of slavery (initially retained, now planned to be changed).[26] Oxford University hosted formal and informal debates over whether the statue of Cecil Rhodes should be removed from the facade of Oriel College (it remains).[27] Princeton hosted a similar debate as to the legacy of Woodrow Wilson, his racist views, and the naming of its Woodrow Wilson School of Public and International Affairs (it, too, remains).[28]

***

The topics of safe spaces, trigger warnings, microaggressions, and disinviting speakers are all worth thinking about carefully, but they are neither the main point nor the end point of the conversation about free speech and diversity on campus. These topics need not be set up as litmus tests for administrators for whether they are "for" diversity or "for" free expression, separating people into one camp or another. In every academic community, we must strike a delicate balance between competing perspectives and values. We must do so here, too.

The other reason to avoid quick solutions and to take a deep breath is that many descriptions of this particular tension are often far overblown.[29] The culture war about free expression and diversity has become a proxy fight for other issues. The headlines, even from mainstream news outlets, that today's college students comprise a "generation that hates speech" contradict the facts, which tell a different story.

Young people overwhelmingly continue to support the First Amendment. In fact, the evidence suggests that support for the First Amendment among them is going up, not down. Professor Ken Dautrich of the University of Connecticut designed a survey of high school students in 2004 and, commissioned by the Knight Foundation, has fielded it a total of five times since then (Dautrich 2006, 2007, 2011, 2014, and 2016; also see Dautrich and Yalof 2006, 2007, as well as Dautrich, Yalof, and López 2008). In the 2016 survey of high school students, 91 percent of students said that people should be able to express unpopular opinions, up by 8 percent from a survey in 2004. While adults (76 percent) were twice as likely as students (37 percent) in 2006 to disagree that "the First Amendment goes too far in guaranteeing free expression rights," student support has steadily increased to 56 percent (while adult views remain at similar levels to a decade ago). The bottom line: student support for the First Amendment across the past six surveys has been growing steadily. In nearly every indicator in Dautrich's surveys, student support for free expression rights appears robust and is heading up, not down. One of the survey's most compelling findings is that there is a correlation between students who express support for free expression and those who get their news on mobile devices and engage extensively in social media usage.[30]

College students, likewise, continue to express support for free expression on campus and beyond. A 2016 survey of 3,000 college students in the United States, commissioned by the Knight Foundation and the Newseum Institute, showed that students are highly confident about the security of each of the five First Amendment rights, particularly freedom of the press (81 percent), freedom to petition the government (76 percent), and freedom of speech (73 percent). In each of these areas, college students had a stronger sense of the security of the First Amendment than a corresponding group of adult respondents. By a margin of 78 to 22 percent in that same survey, more students said colleges should expose students to all types of speech rather than prohibit biased or offensive speech. Seventy-three percent of students believed that a school should not be able to restrict expression of potentially offensive political viewpoints. A full 90 percent of respondents said that freedom of the press is just as important to democracy as it was twenty years ago, if not more so.[31] A smaller survey of 800 students on campus reached a similar finding in 2015: over 80 percent of college students said that freedom of speech should be either less limited on college campuses or there should be no difference compared to society at large.[32]

These findings hardly suggest an entire "generation" that "hates speech." The fact that a subset of student activists who, in their enthusiasm for a cause or when caught up in the emotion of a fraught interaction, call for new restrictions on speech does not represent the views of an entire generation—a generation of students learning about how society operates and forming their views about essential issues such as free expression. (Others take a dimmer view of student views on free expression: leading scholars Howard Gillman and Erwin Chemerinsky were "surprised by the often unanimous willingness" of students they were teaching "to support efforts to restrict and punish a wide range of expression." I certainly support their conclusion: "Don't mock or ignore students' lack of support for free speech; teach them.")[33]

The problematic aspect of the 2016 survey data that gives rise to concerns by free speech advocates has to do with the way young people think hate speech should be handled, not with the general support for the First Amendment. Sixty-nine percent of college students said that schools should be able to restrict slurs and other intentionally harmful language. Fifty-four percent of respondents said that the climate on campus prevents them from saying what they believe because others might find it offensive. The split among institutions on approaches to hate speech on campus—between those that regulate hate speech through campus speech codes and those that hew more closely to the First Amendment as the guide—mirrors the split among students.[34] These data point to something hopeful: there is much room for good teaching to be done on this topic.[35]

With seriousness of purpose, a high degree of tolerance, and deep empathy as the mode of operation, it is possible to embrace diversity and free expression at the same time. Rather than fanning the flames of a heated national cultural war in public statements, academic administrators can build on the strong support for free expression and diversity to bring people together and to educate. When structured with care, these processes can inform and teach as they resolve conflicts on campus—turning flashpoints into periods of introspection and learning.

3   The Case for Diversity

As a high school senior from Texas, Abigail Fisher applied to the University of Texas at Austin for admission to its undergraduate program. In 2008, the university denied her admission. Fisher, in turn, sued the university for violating her constitutional rights. Among other things, she argued that the university owed her a duty under the Equal Protection Clause that it did not uphold by admitting minority students who had performed less well than she had on tests and in school. This violation, Fisher argued, arose as a result of the university's use of race as one of the criteria by which it reached its admissions decisions. Fisher claimed that she and other similarly situated white applicants had suffered harm as a consequence of this policy, which should be deemed unconstitutional.[1]

The legal battle that ensued took eight years and several levels of courts to bring to a close. The university prevailed at more or less every turn. The first court to take up Fisher's claim, a federal court in Texas, found that the university was permitted to use race as a criterion for admission in the way that it had. Fisher appealed all the way up to the U.S. Supreme Court. The justices agreed to hear her case.

In 2013, in the first of two rulings—called *Fisher I* for short—the Supreme Court again supported the decision, but sent it back to the lower court for further consideration under a tougher standard: "strict scrutiny." After the lower court reaffirmed the previous decision, Fisher's case made it back up to the U.S. Supreme Court. In 2016, the Court—in a decision called *Fisher II*—again affirmed the university's right to use race as a criterion in admissions. Eight years into the dispute, and well after Fisher had graduated from another college, the Supreme Court squarely affirmed the use of race as a criterion in college admissions.[2]

The *Fisher* case is important on many levels. It is an important counterpart to *Brown v. Board of Education* in 1954, which cleared the way for integration of the public school system in America.[3] *Fisher* built on previous Supreme Court cases, in particular the twin matters of *Grutter v. Bollinger* and *Gratz v. Bollinger*, which pertained to the University of Michigan's affirmative action policies in admissions.[4] Together, these holdings by the Supreme Court established a firm legal basis for the use of race as a factor in college admissions processes, so long as the universities follow a series of steps in doing so.

The *Fisher* case is also important because it prompted public consideration of the merits of diversity in education. Looked at from that angle, the case was about whether the University of Texas at Austin had articulated sound enough educational reasons to favor the kind of diversity it sought—in this case, to admit a certain number of otherwise qualified minority students even if those students did not have academic qualifications that were, on their face, higher than those of all other applicants, including Fisher.

A powerful case for the merits of diversity in education is embedded in the many arguments that the courts heard over those several years. Much of this case for diversity can be found in the courts' written opinions. In particular, the collection of more than 100 amicus briefs filed in the Fisher cases is an extraordinary source of data and powerful argumentation about why diversity matters and how it connects to the learning process.

Though the legal process took many twists and turns over eight years, all the courts fundamentally agreed on one thing: diversity is good for learning and good for democracy in the long run. The Supreme Court summarized the reasons that it found compelling: "e.g., ending stereotypes, promoting 'cross-racial understanding,' preparing students for 'an increasingly diverse workforce and society,' and cultivating leaders with 'legitimacy in the eyes of the citizenry.'" These reasons, among others, amounted to a sufficiently strong rationale for the use of race by the university in its admissions process. Let's start with these four reasons as core to the case for diversity in education.

***

The first compelling argument for diversity: ending stereotypes. All humans grow up with biases. Regardless of our race or ethnicity, our faith or our gender, we are biased toward and against other human beings. The body of research on this topic is so strong as to be incontrovertible. As Mahzarin Banaji and Anthony Greenwald describe in their book *Blindspot: Hidden Biases of Good People*, we all harbor what they call implicit biases, no matter who we are. (If you are still skeptical on this score, there is a test you can take online that may well convince you: https://implicit.harvard.edu/implicit.) These biases derive from many sources, including our upbringing and the stereotypes we encounter through our everyday lives—in the media, among our friends and family, and in our schools and workplaces.[5]

One legitimate goal of the educational process is to end stereotypes, which are harmful in multiple respects. They hurt those who suffer from the bias of others. Stereotypes also limit the understanding of those of us (which is to say all of us) who harbor them. Stereotyping means that we do not see the essential humanity in one another, fail to connect with those different from us, and lose out on the many advantages of mutual understanding across the lines of difference.

Large or small, the effects of stereotyping reach far beyond school and university walls to national and international policy matters. Claude Steele, a prominent sociologist, points to various forms of stereotype threat.[6] In his book *Whistling Vivaldi: And Other Clues to How Stereotypes Affect Us*, Steele describes the experience of Brent Staples, then a graduate student at the University of Chicago. Staples discovered that he was treated very differently depending on whether he whistled Vivaldi while walking in the evening through the Hyde Park neighborhood of Chicago where he lived. When he did not, white passersby often crossed to the other side of the street or otherwise acted afraid; when he did, he was instead occasionally met with smiles.[7] This same stereotyping leads to more serious harms when applied to groups of people within a population. For instance, the disproportionate number of African Americans stopped for certain infractions, incarcerated in the United States, or harmed through police violence, can be traced both to structural inequities in the nation's history and to implicit bias on the part of those involved in the justice system (while acknowledging those very many law enforcement officers who have every good intention in carrying out their public duties).[8]

Diversity in an educational setting is one means of ending stereotypes and reversing the effects of this implicit bias across society. A young person who grows up in a completely homogeneous environment, attends a homogeneous school, and plays in homogeneous groups will have little opportunity to examine or test their understanding of ingrained biases and stereotypes. Research shows that when diverse groups of students work in teams to solve problems, their collaboration can help reduce stereotyping. This problem-solving approach can work even better than programs focused on talking across differences. Schools and universities are ideal places for these problem-solving environments to thrive and serve our students.[9] A well-structured, diverse educational environment provides the opportunity to address the negative effects of bias and stereotyping locally on campuses and in society at large.

***

The second compelling argument for diversity: promoting cross-racial understanding. The national discord that followed a series of deaths of African Americans, leading to the establishment of the #BlackLivesMatter movement and the #SayHerName movement, has made plain the deep need for sustained work toward cross-racial harmony in the United States.[10] In 2016, 70 percent of Americans reported that "race relations are generally bad," among the highest levels of race-based discord in decades.[11] The need for improved cross-racial understanding, in America and around the world, is urgent, especially in the context of the 2016 presidential election between Donald Trump and Hillary Clinton that has put a spotlight on racial differences in the United States.[12]

Race is not the only form of difference that matters; the frame adopted by the Supreme Court might reasonably be extended to include ethnicity, faith, gender, and sexual orientation, among other differences. Better interfaith understanding, connections across lines of gender and sexuality, and other forms of bridging are needed just as badly on a global scale.

Campuses have long been the site of discussion about race and difference. Cross-racial discussion can take multiple forms. It can be enormously fruitful and educationally valuable, but if structured poorly, it can result in divisions among students and faculty. Campuses can develop climates that are positive and supportive of all community members; campuses can also take a negative turn, dividing community members and dissuading prospective applicants from joining the community. In a campus environment, educators can help to structure spaces in which students rub elbows with people of many different backgrounds and are able to share ideas in a way that can be less natural at other stages of life. Those who have lived in campus dormitories, for instance, often reflect on the enduring power of "late-night bull sessions" in which young people of different backgrounds bat around the ideas of the day. These times—perhaps to the detriment of getting their homework done—can help build life-long bonds and empathy between people who might otherwise never meet.

The strongest educational communities are ones where participants choose a path grounded in mutual understanding, inclusivity, and respect. Students and faculty can learn by truly listening to one another, learning about one another's background, and finding common ground across differences. In a simpler sense, cross-racial understanding can lead to friendships and connections that may be enormously valuable on a person-to-person level.

These educational gains in understanding one another across difference—racial and otherwise—cannot happen consistently without a diverse student and faculty body. One of the key issues before the Court in the *Fisher* case turned on this question of what it meant, exactly, to have a diverse community: what a critical mass might look like in terms of people from different backgrounds. The university argued, successfully in the end, that it had sufficiently defined what it meant to have a "diverse" community, while Fisher's lawyers argued that the university was too vague in this respect. The Court ultimately sided with the university, which argued that its admissions office had a good and sufficient sense of what it meant to have the kind of diversity on campus that drives educational benefits. Scholars have also argued that there is such a thing as communities that are *too* diverse, so it may be that the question is not how much diversity is "enough" but rather how much is "optimal."[13]

The ability to talk to one another and to live with one another despite our differences is one of the most important skills people can learn in schools and universities. It is itself a form of excellence that students need to develop. Schools cannot pursue this form of excellence without an intentionally diverse community in which students and faculty are educating one another across differences.

Competency in diversity is essential to humans thriving in an increasingly global, interconnected world. Disputes, big and small, have been fought over racial, ethnic, and faith-based misunderstandings throughout history. The rancor in America on topics related to race in 2016, during the political season and on campuses, is but one example that demonstrates the importance of this work. Whether in the long-running struggle over territory in the Middle East and North Africa that extends to the present day, the Holocaust in the middle of the twentieth century, or countless sectarian disputes around the world, an absence of cross-racial harmony and understanding leads to atrocities and unmeasurable harms. Empathy across difference, brought about through diversity in education, offers the promise of saving lives by reducing armed conflict, within and across states.

***

The third compelling argument for diversity: preparing students for an increasingly diverse workforce and society. Education is in part about preparing young people to succeed in their professional and civic lives. Our schools ought to ensure that students are prepared to thrive in jobs available to them when they graduate. Educators also strive to ensure that our graduates are well prepared to serve as good citizens who can help our society thrive as a whole. In the twenty-first century, diversity is an essential element in both of these respects.

The workforce that our young graduates are entering is more complex, more diverse, and more interconnected at a global scale than ever before. On the most obvious level, students who have experienced only a homogeneous school environment will find themselves unprepared when they reach a workplace vastly more diverse than the communities in which they have grown up. A student who has only interacted with those of a certain gender, for instance, might find it challenging to work alongside those of another gender. Diversity in schools makes possible interaction with those who have a different perspective before entering the workforce and learning these lessons on the job.

The workers of the twenty-first century will also need to be more skilled in collaboration than workers in the past. Economies around the world are switching away from manufacturing and agriculture toward services and knowledge work. The types of jobs that are growing quickly tend to require knowledge workers, almost always organized in teams. Unlike the manual labor of the past, these knowledge-oriented jobs call for a high level of interaction among people to accomplish their assigned tasks. Schools and universities have responded to these changes by emphasizing work in teams, project-based assignments, and collaborative forms of assessment. The late-night informal engagement between students in residence halls may pay off in this respect, too.

Diversity in schools and universities helps students work well in teams. Some of these gains come in diverse classroom settings or in purposefully designed diversity workshops and forums. The gains often come from informal, unplanned interactions in diverse environments. Students playing on a sports team with classmates from different backgrounds come to appreciate the strengths of their teammates. Musicians who play instruments or sing in a chorus or musical with those of different race or faith backgrounds gain new skills. It may well be that those skills, developed on the court or in the auditorium, will prove to be among the most valuable abilities learned during a student's education when it comes to preparing for the workforce. Our schools, at every level, ought to make this type of learning central to their work.

***

The fourth compelling argument for diversity: cultivating leaders with legitimacy in the eyes of the citizenry. We educate young people in part to prepare them to take on positions of leadership in adulthood. The Supreme Court considered the need to cultivate leaders deemed "legitimate" in the eyes of the citizenry one of the values of a diverse student body. According to the University of Texas at Austin, the educational goals of diversity include the "acquisition of competencies required of future leaders."[14]

Leadership takes many forms. The leaders of a democratic state ought to reflect the racial, ethnic, gender, faith-based, and sexual composition of the people at large. A truly equitable and inclusive state would involve leaders who have different levels of ability in various respects, including the inability to see, hear, read, and so forth. Few states have ever truly managed to create this particular form of legitimacy. If members of a particular group are systematically denied key educational opportunities, then it is unlikely that they will make it through the gauntlet between the time they leave school and the time they try to assume senior leadership positions. The point is not that it is impossible for members of that group to succeed in leadership, but rather that it is less likely to the extent that they have been excluded from the most selective educational institutions. For instance, up through the 2016 election, candidates who were white, male, heterosexual, and Christian were more likely to be elected president of the United States than those who were not. It was possible for a mixed-race man to be elected, as Barack Obama was in 2008 and again in 2012, but he was the exception to the rule. The same is true outside of civic leadership—the skills gained in good educational institutions help in climbing the corporate ladder, too, and in attaining a leadership position in a for-profit or nonprofit organization.

In these respects, race and ethnicity are important elements of diversity, though far from the only ones. Consider, for instance, people who have served in the military or come from military families. If those who have served, or have parents who have served, are less likely to be admitted to highly selective educational institutions, they may be less likely to attain positions of leadership outside the military itself. Legitimacy in the eyes of the citizenry would surely be served by the inclusion of young people from military families in positions of civic leadership, regardless of their race, gender, or sexuality.

This fourth reason invoked by the Supreme Court in *Fisher II* links the educational benefits of diversity directly to civic and political life. If educational institutions do their job in educating a diverse array of students, the state as a whole will benefit when those students graduate and assume the mantle of leadership over time. To the extent that all groups in the state see themselves represented in positions of leadership across all facets of society, the polity at large stands to benefit from the strength of those ties and the engagement in civic life that can flow from it. This final point links the educational benefits of diversity to the civic and economic benefits that diversity can bring to a society.

***

The Supreme Court in *Fisher II* mentioned only a handful of the possible arguments in favor of diversity. One can almost hear the justices and their clerks, writing for the majority, leave off that section of their opinion with "and so forth" after describing the first four reasons. The several arguments that the Court seized on fall into the category of functional reasons for diversity. These reasons are not wrong; they are, however, an incomplete catalog of all the possible rationales for diversity in education, not to mention in workplaces, on sports teams, and in society at large. While logically compelling, this list of reasons has a bit of a clinical, bloodless feel to it.

The Court focused largely on educational outcomes for all students, including those in the majority (including, prospectively, Fisher herself) in its reasoning. An additional rationale for diversity is that it enables better educational outcomes for a subset of students, in particular those who come from communities historically underrepresented in elite educational institutions. Common sense suggests that having a critical mass of minority students lessens the alienation and loneliness that can lead to poorer educational outcomes among students from those groups. Social science research backs up this claim. These cognitive benefits, even if enjoyed primarily by a subset of students, matter to individuals, groups, and society as a whole.

Diversity is linked to the positive development of social and emotional growth, as well as cognitive gains. One way to see this growth is through the connection between diversity and the development of a sense of "voice" in young people. Mina Huang, writing of the power of diversity in her educational experience as a student at Wilfrid Laurier University in 2015, said: "Diversity gives people a voice. Diversity empowers people to be expressive without feeling outnumbered. It allows us to raise a hand in disagreement with a majority of our peers while presenting the opportunity to see things from a different perspective."[15] As young people grow and develop a sense of their personal and social identities, the diversity in their learning community matters to their social and emotional well-being.

***

There are other types of arguments for diversity beyond the functional reasons favored by the Supreme Court in the *Fisher II* majority opinion. Some of these reasons are aspirational, such as fulfillment of the promise—yet unrealized—of the American dream for all citizens. As every schoolchild in America knows, the basis for the founding of the United States includes soaring rhetoric along these lines: "We hold these truths to be self-evident, that all men are created equal." (The Declaration of Independence, drafted by the slaveholder Thomas Jefferson, is hardly a model of inclusivity, of course; one has to set aside the part about the "men" and the later references to "merciless Indian Savages" to celebrate the message about equality.)[16] That shared aspiration, of a state in which all people are in fact treated equally, relies on a commitment to diversity in education as a part of the process.

Other arguments are moral and ethical. Given the way certain groups of people have been treated historically, programs that favor diversity are a moral necessity. These moral and ethical arguments rest on the structural effects of inequality in the past. Today's society, in turn, should respond with the ambitious diversification of educational institutions as one in a series of efforts to reverse the effects of systemic injustice over time.

Most of the well-established, elite educational institutions in the United States admitted predominantly white, male applicants of Anglo-Saxon heritage for generations. Over the course of the twentieth century, that pattern changed, slowly and in fits and starts, and admission was extended to women, people of Jewish ancestry, people of color, and people who were openly members of the LBGTQIA+ community. Those in the majority have a moral obligation to render homogeneous institutions more diverse and inclusive over time, much as the Supreme Court told public schools in 1954, in *Brown v. Board of Education,* that they must no longer remain segregated. The *Fisher* case pointed to that dispute more than fifty years later by showing exactly how to accomplish equality in this respect.

Diversity in education is a powerful means of addressing these aspirational and moral claims. One need not agree with all these arguments for diversity in order to support it; in fact, the case for diversity might require only one of the many plausible rationales, and any of them is strong enough to overcome the counterpoint to diversity, namely the argument in favor of homophily. In focusing on education one invests in the future, in the human potential of our young people. The best way to overcome the structural racism and other-ism of the past is to invest in those who will lead the society's institutions into the future.

The case for diversity extends far beyond the realm of education. Diversity can enhance the work of for-profit and not-for-profit firms of most types imaginable, which is a reason why many firms pursue diversity in a variety of dimensions. At the level of complex systems, diversity is a driver of innovation and productivity. Diversity can render such systems—including, importantly, cities—more robust over time.

The case for diversity in education stops with neither diversity alone nor education alone. Diversity in the numerical sense is necessary but not sufficient—the educational process works well only when leaders throughout the community build on and drive a diverse community toward meaningful levels of equity and inclusion. This distinction pulls apart the *structural diversity* of having certain numbers of community members who self-identify in different ways—often a first phase of work—and the *interaction diversity* that occurs among people on the campus in positive and enriching contexts. Diversity in education is even stronger when connected to diversity outside the classroom walls, when it is deeply connected to diversity in the workplace and in civic life.

Diversity without a meaningful effort to make something valuable out of it—to ensure that the people and institutions benefit from it—will not do much of anything other than perhaps cause resentment. Some point to the limits of diversity in educational institutions and argue that it is inadequate to the task. The journalist Ta-Nehisi Coates, for instance, has extended the moral argument beyond the need for diversity in institutions to a call for reparations.[17] Others state that the United States can only move forward after confronting and addressing the debts of slavery, Jim Crow, and additional harms to African Americans and the Native Americans who predated European settlers in the United States. The case for diversity is in fact a case for much bigger changes to the structure of our institutions.

While most research points to the substantial educational and democratic benefits of diversity, it can also come with costs. Diversity can lead to additional conflicts among community members unused to interacting with people from different backgrounds. Initially, as communities become more diverse, concerns can arise over lower levels of trust among community members, self-segregation and isolation, or avoidance of opposing or critical viewpoints. Mere contact or exposure to persons from other backgrounds may not increase tolerance unless it happens in an environment with a positive campus climate. Schools and universities that do not have strong cultural norms of equity and cooperation between diverse groups—particularly across race, gender, and sexuality—often experience tension as their communities become more diverse. Knowledge of different groups and cultures, the opportunity to form friendships across racial, ethnic, and religious backgrounds, and seeing teachers supportive of cross-cultural and interethnic relationships can also increase empathy among students—but only when these activities are valued and supported. These potential drawbacks do not outweigh the manifold benefits of diversity, but academic leaders must take them seriously.[18]

***

Diversity, equity, and inclusion work in education could not be more pressing than it is today, in the wake of a contentious election that broke down so sharply along racial and ethnic lines. A strong majority of white men favored a winning candidate (Donald J. Trump) who openly criticized Muslims and Mexican

Americans, while the losing candidate (Hillary R. Clinton) drew support from an overwhelming percentage of African-American and Hispanic voters (of all genders). The outcome of the election led to a spate of racial incidents on campuses and in other communities, which in turn have shone a spotlight on the massive gulfs separating groups of U.S. citizens.[19] Similar patterns have emerged in elections in Western Europe in recent years. It is incontrovertible that today's democratic systems are strained along the lines of racial and ethnic difference; given the demographic trends, we must take seriously our ability to address root causes of these strains.

The importance of diversity in our public life is only going to grow, not diminish, over time. The group of young people coming of age in the early twenty-first century is the "generation of diversity." A study by Brookings Institution senior fellow William Frey claims that "racial diversity will be the most defining and impactful characteristic of the millennial generation."[20] Educational institutions must not miss the challenges and opportunities posed by the demographic evolution of the United States, from a majority white country to one with no specific majority racial group by 2044.[21] Demographic trends also suggest that the changes will continue throughout this generation's lifetime, with, for instance, people of Asian descent surpassing those of Latin American descent by 2055 and with immigration from Africa growing sharply.[22]

Diversity on campuses from the standpoint of the *Fisher* decision did not explicitly include diversity of political opinion. I return to the topic of heterodox political communities in the conclusion to this book, but I believe that advocates of diversity—and I seek to be among them—would do well to consider the benefits of striving for a diversity of political views on campus alongside other forms of diversity. Political viewpoints do fall into another category than, say, race; the former is plainly more easily malleable than the latter, for instance. They are also different insofar as certain underrepresented minorities have suffered the effects of structural racism for a long time, whereas those with most political views have not. I include the notion of a range of political viewpoints here not because the moral arguments are comparable, but because many of the same learning benefits can accrue from diversity of views as can accrue from diversity of other sorts. In a divided nation or culture, as we observe in the United States of 2016, the connection across political divides, among well-meaning people, would surely be valuable in certain ways to individuals and to the community at large.

Educational institutions are not the only places that need to focus on diversity and inclusion in times of dramatic demographic change, but they are important places to begin. Young people living in academic communities are likely to be highly effective in garnering the benefits of diversity. That does not mean that all efforts should focus on elite universities, such as the University of Texas at Austin in Fisher's case, or the University of Michigan Law School in those of Grutter and Gratz. The case for diversity extends across all forms of schooling in our society, in the spirit of what the *Brown v. Board of Education* decision told Americans in 1954 about the need for racial integration.

As crucial as it is, the case for diversity is not the sole topic of this book. There is a deep connection between the benefits to be gained through diversity in education and those resulting from a culture of free expression on campuses. As the University of Texas at Austin claimed in its defense to Fisher, and as the Supreme Court agreed in its opinion in *Fisher II*, a central element of education—and of diversity in education—is to promote "a robust exchange of ideas."[23] Diversity, in other words, is essential to freedom of expression. Pursued in concert, diversity and free expression both become stronger and more important. Together, diversity and freedom of expression offer the greatest promise of accomplishing our essential educational and civic goals as a democracy.

4   The Case for Free Expression

Over the course of the nineteenth century, the Russian czars enacted a series of harshly anti-Semitic laws, policies, and practices. Between 1908 and 1913, five young Jewish people—Jacob Abrams, Mollie Steimer, Hyman Lachowsky, Samuel Lipman, and Jacob Schwartz—fled Russia for New York's East Harlem neighborhood. They sought a new life in America, as so many others did, believing in the promise of political and religious freedom.

From their new home in New York, Abrams and his colleagues took up the causes of socialism and anarchism. Abrams and friends vocally supported the rise of the Bolsheviks and the effort to bring down the czar's government in Russia. After the Bolsheviks succeeded in overthrowing the czar and coming to power, they entered into a peace treaty with the Germans in 1917. The next summer, the United States sent troops to the Russian borders, near Vladivostok and Murmansk. The purported reason for these military maneuvers was to maintain an Eastern front against the Germans, the United States' adversaries in the First World War.

To Abrams and his colleagues, however, these maneuvers by the United States had nothing to do with Germany and everything to do with opposing the Russian Revolution, to which they had by this time become devoted. Abrams and his friends printed up two leaflets, one in English and another in Yiddish. Both leaflets called for a general strike by the workers of the United States. The leaflet in English signed off with the words: "Awake! Awake, you Workers of the World! REVOLU-TIONISTS." The leaflet in Yiddish focused on Russian emigrants, urging them to "spit in the face of the false, hypocritic [*sic*] pro-paganda" of the Americans.[1]

Military police arrested Abrams and his colleagues for their allegedly treasonous activities in producing and disseminating the two leaflets. At the end of their first trial, Judge Henry DeLa-mar Clayton found them guilty of conspiring to violate the Sedi-tion Act of 1918 and sentenced them to three to twenty years in prison.

The case came before the U.S. Supreme Court on appeal. Abrams and his fellow defendants raised a First Amendment defense, claiming that they had been denied their right to free expression. In 1919, a majority of the Supreme Court justices denied their claims. The justices in the majority referred to recently discussed, similar cases, where the justices had found no recognizable free speech protection.

Two Supreme Court justices disagreed with the majority in the *Abrams* case. Justice Oliver Wendell Holmes Jr. wrote a dis-senting opinion with which Justice Louis Brandeis concurred. The Holmes dissent in *Abrams* immediately provoked strong opinions, both for and against. It continues to be one of the most famous opinions written by a U.S. Supreme Court jus-tice. The power of this dissent is all the more striking for the fact that it was written for the losing side in this particular debate.

In his dissent, Holmes wrote that he supported the right of Abrams and his colleagues to publish the leaflets and that the state should not have the power to stop them from doing so. The entirety of Holmes's dissent is worth reading, but at its core, he wrote: "The ultimate good desired is better reached by free trade in ideas—that the best test of truth is the power of the thought to get itself accepted in the competition of the market."[2]

Holmes referred to this idea as the "theory of our Constitution." According to him, "It is an experiment, as all life is an experiment. ... While that experiment is part of our system I think that we should be eternally vigilant against attempts to check the expression of opinions that we loathe and believe to be fraught with death, unless they so imminently threaten immediate interference with the lawful and pressing purposes of the law that an immediate check is required to save the country."[3] Holmes set a very high bar—"imminent threat"—for the instances in which speech might be justifiably curtailed. He also linked this strong level of protection of speech, even loathsome speech, with the very theory of the American system of government.

As famous as it is today, Holmes's dissent in *Abrams* came as a surprise to his contemporaries who followed these matters closely. Holmes had agreed with the majority in a series of previous cases in which the Court decided that the government had a greater power to suppress speech in wartime than during times of peace. But by the time the *Abrams* case came around, he had reached a different view—or perhaps saw the facts in *Abrams* differently than the facts in the previous cases.[4]

Holmes's views were brilliantly expressed and immediately praised as historic and likely to be enduring. But they were not original. His metaphor of "free trade in ideas" —later repeated as the "marketplace-of-ideas" doctrine—appeared in John Milton's *Areopagitica* in 1644: "And though all the winds of doctrine were let loose to play upon the earth, so Truth be in the field, we do injuriously by licensing and prohibiting to misdoubt her strength. Let her and Falsehood grapple; who ever knew Truth put to the worse in a free and open encounter?"[5]

The case for free expression can be made in many ways. Some reasons for free expression are more compelling than others. In the American context, the argument in favor of free expression often runs along the lines of Holmes's dissent in *Abrams* and Milton's *Areopagitica* hundreds of years before. This line of reasoning has come to be known in shorthand as the "marketplace-of-ideas" rationale for free expression. A free and open encounter in the public marketplace, the argument goes, is the only way for the best ideas to emerge. This approach to the free expression of ideas ensures that the people making choices—whether voters choosing among possible representatives or representatives choosing among possible laws or policies—have in front of them the full range of potential options.

The general argument that free expression leads to the truth is good up to a point—in a theoretical sense, it is a powerful line of reasoning. When a listener can compare ideas side by side, both made persuasively, then she or he is more likely to be able to come to a sound conclusion than if only one view were developed and shared. In 1860, Frederick Douglass, the leading nineteenth-century abolitionist, made an argument along these lines: "To suppress free speech is a double wrong. It violates the rights of the hearer as well as those of the speaker."[6] As Douglass pointed out, both the speaker and the listener matter and each might benefit from the expression of free speech in the search for the truth. When permitted to try out expressing various ideas, the speaker, too, is more likely to arrive at a truthful statement over time.

The difficulty with the marketplace-of-ideas metaphor—or, more broadly, the "truth-seeking model" of free expression—is that it is essentially laissez-faire in its operation. In practice, even in a stable democracy, some speakers and some hearers have more power than others. Myriad forms of inequality can come into play: unequal voice, unequal access to education, and unequal ability to participate in this marketplace of ideas (when, for example, focusing on more basic human needs such as obtaining food and shelter takes priority).

The theory is not altogether wrong. It is still favored by some theorists. For instance, libertarians who favor the laissez-faire model of economics might also favor the marketplace-of-ideas metaphor when it comes to speech. The theory is, however, constrained by reality, as its critics rightly point out. The Holmesian line of reasoning remains important, but it is no longer the only or the dominant rationale for free expression.

***

In a free country, tongues likewise should be free.
—Desiderius Erasmus, *Education of a Christian Prince*, 1516[7]

Before considering some of the other arguments in favor of free expression, let's step back in time. Long before Abrams and his fellow anarchists tested the strength of the First Amendment during the First World War, the right to free expression had been giving rise to controversy. The right to free expression extends back hundreds of years, well before the founding of the United States. The Magna Carta includes hints of modern-day rights of free expression in the thirteenth century. The English Bill of Rights in the late seventeenth century referenced speech rights, as did the Declaration of the Rights of Man during the French Revolution at the end of the eighteenth century. The source of the right to free expression lay in the "natural rights," enjoyed at least by fully enfranchised men. To most people thinking and writing about it at the time, that meant that the right to free expression came from God. In the United States, the right to free expression is enshrined in the First Amendment to the Constitution. The First Amendment, enacted in 1791, is part of the Bill of Rights. The right to free expression is one of five related rights enshrined in the First Amendment. The amendment reads, in its entirety: "Congress shall make no law respecting an establishment of religion, or prohibiting the free exercise thereof; or abridging the freedom of speech, or of the press; or the right of the people peaceably to assemble, and to petition the government for a redress of grievances."[8] If you read it again with care, you will notice that the First Amendment establishes that *Congress* shall not make a law that abridges the "freedom of speech." This statement appears to be simple, but it is not. It turns out to be very complicated.

One way this right to freedom of speech is complicated is the set of actors to which it is applied. If one were to read the First Amendment as plain English, the answer is straightforward: the rule applies exclusively to the Congress, the legislative arm of the U.S. federal government. Over time, through interpretation by the courts, this restriction has come to be applied to any "state actor." The list of state actors today means most, if not all, state and municipal government agencies. Some of the most challenging cases have involved instances in which the restriction on abridging speech can cover those private entities that are not the state but act like the state—for instance, the owners of a company town in 1940s Alabama and owners of a shopping mall in California in 1980.[9]

What is also left unsaid by the First Amendment is to whom it does *not* apply. Except under rare circumstances, private actors are not bound by the amendment. When a schoolchild shouts on the playground, "Hey, it's a free country—haven't you ever heard of free speech?," the implication is that no one can tell another person what to say or not to say. That schoolchild, alas, is mistaken. The First Amendment is totally silent on that issue. It does not apply to that schoolchild, or to his or her friend who is causing trouble. The First Amendment is often assumed to do something that it does not: to grant an affirmative right to free expression to all people. Instead, it operates as a restraint on the state, stopping those in authority from making laws that abridge the right to free expression. For the purposes of this book, this is a distinction that makes a great difference: by and large, private institutions are not bound by the First Amendment, whereas public institutions generally are.

Even this explanation of the law of free speech, however, goes too far. In the words of legal and literary scholar Stanley Fish, "There's no such thing as free speech, and it's a good thing, too."[10] Even the First Amendment to the U.S. Constitution, broad and powerful compared to most other constitutional speech protections around the world, has important limits as to the types of speech that are in fact protected.

The state constrains free expression from time to time through law and policy in ways that are consonant with the modern-day understanding of the First Amendment. We call these constraints "time, place and manner" restrictions. There are some times when one cannot say something; there are some places where one cannot say something; and there are some manners in which one cannot say something. The Espionage Act offers a wide-ranging example. It is a crime in the United States to reveal certain things about the military and intelligence operations of the government. First enacted by the Congress in 1917, the Espionage Act has been updated many times and its reach has been debated vigorously. Along with the Sedition Act, under which Abrams and his colleagues were prosecuted, the Espionage Act establishes a substantial carve-out to the First Amendment. Under this reasoning, Edward Snowden, the contractor to the National Security Agency who leaked files about government surveillance, did not enjoy full First Amendment protections according to the U.S. government.

There are other exceptions, perhaps more familiar to the casual observer. Most people are aware that it is unlawful to shout "fire" in a crowded theater; to create a "clear and present danger" by inciting another to do violence; to libel someone; and to publish certain obscene materials. These specific exclusions under U.S. law prove that Fish is right: there is "no such thing" as truly "free" speech, even in the country with some of the world's strongest protections for expression.

To make matters even more complex, we have come to see speech as falling into a hierarchy. Certain speech is given less strong constitutional protection than other forms of expression. For instance, commercial advertising is deemed less worthy of strong constitutional expression than, say, expression of an individual's political views. For this reason, Congress can more easily—and is more likely to—regulate the sending of unsolicited commercial emails ("spam") than it can restrict what a citizen might say on a public street corner about a forthcoming election.

The ambit of the First Amendment is instructive on many levels, but the core point is that its reach is limited in certain ways and in certain instances. While there is a very strong presumption in favor of free expression in the United States—stronger than in most if not all other large countries in the world—it is not an absolute, unfettered right. There are good reasons why expression should be broadly protected, and there are occasionally good reasons why it should be limited. The difficulty, of course, is in figuring out where the lines should be drawn—and when and how to do so—such that individuals and the community at large can derive the maximum benefit with the lowest costs. It is no mean feat.

***

The marketplace-of-ideas argument for free expression is one plausible line of reasoning to resolve this difficulty, but it is not the most compelling argument.

A second argument in support of freedom of expression rests on the autonomy of the individual in the context of a democracy. In a free and open society, the right to free expression enables a human being to flourish, in part by enabling the exploration of one's identity and one's views.[11] This theory has merit particularly against the backdrop of a society in which free expression is denied to some or all members of the community. If a person does not have the opportunity to express himself or herself, it is implausible that they would experience autonomy in their life. The ability to express one's views is essential to a person's development, particularly at a young age—for schoolchildren and university students, say, during adolescence—but truly at any age.

This same line of reasoning might apply to a community just as it does to individuals. Consider a small town where much of the decision making that matters most in a person's life is made at the local level, not at the state or federal level. In the U.S. system of governance, many decisions are assigned to the local level—for instance, the system of taxation that funds the local public school system. The right to free expression is as important to a community developing its autonomy as it is for an individual. For a community to be able to form a collective notion of how to organize itself, all individuals need their right to express a broad range of ideas. The autonomy of the community depends on the autonomy of the individuals that comprise it.

The autonomy rationale is useful up to a point but it, too, comes up against its limits relatively quickly. A primary difficulty with this theory that autonomy is needed for a person to thrive is the notion that one person's flourishing (or a community's flourishing) could lead directly to another person's (or community's) harm. For a white supremacist to have the ability to burn a cross in the yard of a person of color, the state must allow a harm to occur. The "speech act" of burning the cross—surely a form of "expression," albeit an abhorrent one—causes harm to the people of color at whom it is directed. The white supremacist may feel as though he or she is flourishing as a result of this expression, but the target of his or her hatred is unlikely to experience that act as anything other than menacing and spiteful. For every community, there are topics that are taboo or harder to confront than other topics. And in every community, there are individuals who find it appealing to test limits, to press on these tender spots, even at the expense of others.

The conversation around free expression is most fraught, most interesting, and most important at these junctures—situations where the interests of one person infringe on the interests of another. Hate speech, to which I devote a later chapter, is the most obvious and frequent place where this tension arises. Communities must develop specific norms and processes to govern these instances. In some cases, the hateful speech is allowed to continue in the name of autonomy or is hiding behind other justifications of free expression. In communities such as schools and universities, speech codes arise to limit hateful speech or bring about sanctions against those who violate these norms. There will always be those who will use the right to free expression to test taboos and limits for their own purposes—even when this testing is especially harmful to particular subgroups in the community. These tensions make evident the limitations of the autonomy theory of free expression.

***

A third theory, one that gives the greatest power to the free speech argument, is the tolerance theory advanced by legal scholar Lee Bollinger.[12] In his book *The Tolerant Society: Freedom of Speech and Extremist Speech in America*, Bollinger asserts that the most effective way to develop a society tolerant of those from diverse backgrounds is to support a strong form of free expression. Tolerance even for most hate speech serves the long-term purposes of a society, according to Bollinger's theory.

The tolerance theory of free expression allows for empathy toward those with less power and fewer opportunities in a society in multiple respects. To tolerate the speech of a recent Jewish immigrant from Russia with unpopular views in the case of Abrams in 1919, views that made the case for anarchism and socialism would be a powerful thing for a society to accomplish. Even though the immediate result of the Abrams case was that the defendants went to prison, the long-term effect of their speech acts has been one that favors tolerance. There is little chance that any of the five would be convicted today, at least for their speech acts. That may partly be because today's politicians are more accustomed to public criticism than were the leaders at the time of the First World War. The explanation for this change may also lie in the power of the ideas advanced by dissent and a growing belief in the value of pluralism and diversity in any democratic society.

The tolerance theory also provides a lens through which to view the long (and continuing) march for civil and political rights in the United States. The notion of equality and a strong form of free expression developed at key intersections in the country's history. Those who argued in favor of equality and inclusion of all people also, along the way, made the strongest case for the right to free expression.

Once the newly formed United States ratified the Constitution (in votes from 1787 to 1790) and the Bill of Rights (in 1791), the right to free expression existed on paper. The words in the First Amendment that describe that right have never changed. Their meaning in practice, though, has evolved substantially in the centuries since then. Those who have fought for the equality of all women and men in the United States have been among the most powerful activists in favor of the right to free expression.

In the first half of the nineteenth century, slavery persisted in the South and several of the Western states of the United States. The movement for abolition, led by a combination of African-American and white men and women, focused primarily on ending slavery. The abolitionists disagreed as to the precise means of ending slavery—there were at least four major strands of abolitionism by 1850—but they frequently agreed that they needed a right to free expression to achieve their aim.

Frederick Douglass's oration, "A Plea for Free Speech in Boston," is among the most enduring proclamations of the importance of free speech of antebellum United States. Douglass and other abolitionists feared the effect of censorship on the ability of those who opposed slavery to make their case to the public. In Douglass's words:

The world moves slowly, and Boston is much like the world. We thought the principle of free speech was an accomplished fact. Here, if nowhere else, we thought the right of the people to assemble and to express their opinion was secure. Dr. Channing had defended the right, Mr. Garrison had practically asserted the right, and Theodore Parker had maintained it with steadiness and fidelity to the last. But here we are to day contending for what we thought we gained years ago. The mortifying and disgraceful fact stares us in the face, that though Faneuil Hall and Bunker Hill Monument stand, freedom of speech is struck down. No lengthy detail of facts is needed. They are already notorious; far more so than will be wished ten years hence.[13]

In his "Plea," Douglass presaged later debates about the importance of free expression by ensuring a right not only to speak but also to hear opinions that might be outside the mainstream discourse.

The abolitionists also helped to build the linkage between and among the various rights clustered in the First Amendment. The right to free expression arose alongside the other essential rights embedded in the First Amendment: the right to freedom of religion, the right to freedom of the press, the right to peaceable assembly, and the right to petition the government for a redress of grievances. William Lloyd Garrison, one of the leading abolitionists mentioned by Douglass, wrote to a correspondent: "Be assured, I clearly see the manly assertion of the right of free thought, free inquiry, and free speech, as against religious intolerance, theological dogmatism, ecclesiastical authority, Papal and Protestant infallibility."[14] For the abolitionists, support for a strong form of the First Amendment protections meant support for the movement to end slavery. The ideas, words, and actions of the abolitionists point toward the essential connections between free expression and related rights.

The women of nineteenth-century America did not have rights equal to those of men. Among other things, women did not have the right to vote. Those arguing for equal rights for women, led by activists such as Lucretia Mott and the Grimké sisters, met frequently with those who favored the abolition of slavery. They shared ideas and strategies. One strand of thinking that linked the women's rights movement to the abolitionist movement was the importance of free speech. Without a right to free expression, the reasoning went, it would be difficult to make the case for change effectively. While there are exceptions to this pattern, as often happens in history, the primary spokespeople arguing for free expression did so in service of promoting systemic change. Those who sought to stifle the rights of free expression did so in the service of maintaining the status quo— the hegemony of men and of the property-owning whites of the Southern United States.

The case for free expression was important to those fighting for civil rights in the twentieth century, just as it was in the nineteenth century. At the University of California at Berkeley in 1964, campaigns for racial and gender equality gave rise to a renewed movement for free expression. In the words of professor and activist Bettina Aptheker:

On October 1, 1964, hundreds of us surrounded a police car on the Berkeley campus of the University of California and refused to allow the police to arrest Jack Weinberg, a graduate student in mathematics who was "manning" a table for the Congress of Racial Equality on the campus's central Sproul Hall Plaza. We held the car for 32 hours with Jack inside and 950 police massed just outside the campus's main entrance waiting for orders to commence an assault to break us up. Shortly before 7 PM on Friday, October 3, student negotiators led by Mario Savio, who was to become the primary spokesperson for the Movement, had reached an intermediary agreement with the University President. The Free Speech Movement was born.[15]

Roughly a century after the formal end to slavery in the United States, activists for equality found themselves again arguing in favor of a strong form of freedom of expression to be able to make their case effectively. The point of reviewing these examples of progressive reformers as some of the most prominent free speech advocates throughout U.S. history is to highlight the extent to which the right to free expression supports the growth of a stronger and more inclusive society.

Tolerance theory links a commitment to free expression with a commitment to equality. As Frederick Douglass taught us, the key is to focus on the effect of the expression on both the speaker and the listener, and by doing so to strive to become a more tolerant society. The purpose of the right of free expression is thus aligned with the purposes of a more equitable and inclusive society, even as these goals often appear to be at odds with one another.

Today, in the twenty-first century, the use of new media—especially networked digital communications—is putting the idea of freedom of expression to a new test. As Holmes argued in his dissent in the *Abrams* case, the theory of our Constitution is an "experiment." Through our use of new technologies, we are hurtling into yet another experimental age, one in which the speed, persistence, and scale of our communications are potentially less constrained by states, and likely more by corporations, than in the past.

***

When the Internet first hit the mainstream, some argued that it should be a more "free" space than other spaces in the interest of the public good and greater equality. The former Grateful Dead lyricist John Perry Barlow gave voice to this argument in a manifesto titled "A Declaration of Independence of Cyberspace," written at Davos, Switzerland, in February 1996. Barlow wrote:

Cyberspace consists of transactions, relationships, and thought itself, arrayed like a standing wave in the web of our communications. Ours is a world that is both everywhere and nowhere, but it is not where bodies live. We are creating a world that all may enter without privilege or prejudice accorded by race, economic power, military force, or station of birth. We are creating a world where anyone, anywhere may express his or her beliefs, no matter how singular, without fear of being coerced into silence or conformity.[16]

Barlow's Declaration of Independence of Cyberspace became the rallying call for a movement known as "cyberlibertarianism." The great hope of the cyberlibertarians centered on the possibilities of a more equitable, less constrained sphere of life that could be built exclusively online. This movement held out hope for new forms of governance that would operate beyond the reach of governments. The only law that was needed, in Barlow's words, was the "golden rule": that community members would do unto others as they would have done unto themselves.

Barlow also correctly predicted that a combination of actors would embrace this libertarian vision of how to govern this emerging "space" in the absence of a conventional sovereign. As excited as he was about the possibilities of this new environment, he feared corporate and state actors working together to constrain speech for private gain: "Your increasingly obsolete information industries would perpetuate themselves by proposing laws, in America and elsewhere, that claim to own speech itself throughout the world. These laws would declare ideas to be another industrial product, no more noble than pig iron."[17] In Barlow's vision, the online environment would favor free expression over the use of ideas and expression for corporate gain.

Barlow and the cyberlibertarians have not succeeded in realizing their vision. The digital space is governed more or less the same way as other human interactions have been governed in the predigital, analog world. Nonetheless, the words of Barlow's Declaration continue to have rhetorical appeal in making the case for free expression in a fast-changing media environment. And there is no question that the Internet and social media matter when it comes to free expression (and diversity for that matter) in the twenty-first century.

Barlow was prescient in calling attention to the transformative change in the way we think about free expression, given how we communicate using digital devices. At a fundamental level, more people have access to information and knowledge than ever before in human history. Today, billions of people (though not all people) have the ability to publish their ideas freely online, such that anyone on the open Internet can view or hear their speech. Before the Internet, one needed money and power to be able to communicate widely and freely—by owning, for instance, a television network or a publishing company. Though no one is guaranteed an audience, the possibility of reaching large numbers of people is now unprecedented.

The effects of these changes on individuals and communities are only becoming clear with time and they are decidedly mixed. Many people, especially those living under authoritarian regimes, have gained the increased autonomy offered by greater access to information and more opportunities to express themselves freely. Those same people use digital, networked technologies at their peril because oppressive rulers use the same technologies to track their online activities and to jail them for expressing their views publicly.

The use of digital communication also leads to more persistent forms of speech. Much more of our digital communication is recorded for posterity and available for later review than is true of offline speech, which is more ephemeral. When posted on social media, our speech is also networked and can potentially be read, heard, or viewed instantly by any one of the billions of people online.

This reach and persistence has many consequences for speech. For one thing, it means that the potential harms of certain kinds of speech can be greater. If speech that might have been hurtful were never recorded, it would never be encountered by a listener to whom it could have been harmful. Today, that same speech, when recorded and shared broadly, can reach many people who could find it harmful.

Consider the leaflets that Abrams and his colleagues produced during the First World War. In early-twentieth-century New York, those leaflets were likely to reach a limited number of readers in physical proximity to Abrams and his fellow anarchists. A leaflet could of course be reproduced on a printing press or be put on a boat or train and be more widely distributed. But these modes of dissemination were slow and costly, especially when compared to current modes of communication.

What would the activists of the digital era do in Abrams's position? They would perhaps start a hashtag campaign. The supporters of Bernie Sanders's insurgent campaign against Hillary Clinton used many such hashtags—for example, "#Slogans4Hillary," which quickly became the most trending hashtag on Twitter, only hours after activists thrust it into usage.[18] Those who opposed Hillary Clinton's candidacy from the right also used hashtags for negative purposes: #WordsThatDontDescribe-Hillary, for instance.[19] They might have written a blog post, updated a status on Facebook, posted a photo on Instagram, or started a story on Snapchat. Ditto for the activists behind #BlackLivesMatter and #SayHerName. Any of these acts would have cost them no more than whatever they paid for access to the Internet (or be potentially free at, say, a public library). And the reach of their digital activism could have extended to literally billions of people connected to the Internet. This argument about the reach, low cost, and replicability of digital communications has yet to alter materially the way free expression is protected in the United States.

This digital environment frequently lends itself to incivility in interpersonal discourse. People are often less civil to one another when the conversation is mediated digitally than in face-to-face encounters, a phenomenon known as the *disinhibition effect*. Most people who have spent time using new media know how easy it is to forget oneself and hit "send" too quickly on an abrasive email, an obnoxious (even if funny at the time) Tweet, or a witty response on Facebook (that someone might take the "wrong way" without the context of a face-to-face interaction). On social media, for instance, young people will often say something quickly and more harshly than they might in the classroom. They cannot see, or even envision, all the recipients of their speech. They act out of emotion, as they might in the privacy of their own home, even though their speech might reverberate around the world—and persist for the rest of their life in digital form online.[20]

Digital-era activism also differs in the way individuals tend to act when engaged in discourse. For example, the disinhibition effect comes into play in political dialogue. The 2016 presidential election was marked by especially ugly rhetoric online, stoked in particular by Donald Trump and his supporters on Twitter. Democrats were not immune to hurtful online commentary in response, as the characterization of Republican supporters as "deplorables" reverberated through social media. No one had reason to feel especially good about the quality of the online rhetoric in the 2016 election cycle.

In the era of digital media, the effects of speech—hateful speech as well as socially constructive speech—are greater than ever before. The rationale for an empathetic, tolerant society is no less pressing today than before the advent of the Internet and social media. While Barlow's proposal for an extreme form of free expression online has not come to pass, his call to action has underscored the potential for new media to build on the positive effects of free expression for individuals and communities.

***

One does not have to agree with all the arguments for free expression to take the need to protect it seriously. For those who favor a libertarian line of reasoning (whether cyber- or otherwise), the concept of the marketplace of ideas might resonate. For those concerned about redressing the effects of unequal power in society, the need to allow for dissent against the powerful might hold greater force. The right to free expression has enduring importance either way. In an era in which the use of new media is changing the environment for politics and human discourse, it is increasingly important that we clarify our thinking on the degree of free expression we wish to support in our society.

At no time in U.S. history has the right to free expression been unfettered. This right is regularly weighed against other important principles, such as individual safety, national security, and equality. The claims of those who believe diversity initiatives are more important than free expression ought to be considered in light of the many competing claims for when and how the absolute right to free expression is curtailed. The right to free expression deserves support by those who seek progressive ends as well as those with a conservative agenda: it underpins our ability to function as a democratic society, regardless of who has the upper hand at any given moment. The interests of diversity and free expression point in the same direction, toward a more tolerant and democratic society in which we support the flourishing of our citizens, a genuine search for the truth, and the conditions for sound civic decision making—with careful limitations against the most dangerous speech at the margins.

5 The Hard Problem of Hate Speech

Hate speech has bedeviled communities for a very long time. In democratic societies, few people believe that political views should be suppressed today. The trouble comes when one person utters words that he or she believes are protected political speech and someone hearing the same words believes it is hate speech. In the modern era, the U.S. Supreme Court has interpreted the First Amendment as protecting both political speech and most hate speech from government restriction. The United States stands essentially alone in this respect. Most other democracies—Canada and much of northern Europe, for instance—expressly restrict hate speech through national legislation even when they have broad protections for other kinds of speech.

Campuses today are split in their approach to hate speech, just as nations are. According to the latest annual survey by the Foundation for Individual Rights in Education (FIRE), 39 percent of the U.S. colleges and universities they reviewed receive a "red light" mark for campus rules for "clearly and substantially" restricting free expression on campus. Many (though far from all) of these restrictions take the form of rules against hate speech.[1] Other campuses, according to FIRE, hew more closely to the First Amendment approach when it comes to regulating speech. (When I refer to "hate speech," I adopt the *Oxford English Dictionary*'s definition: "speech expressing hatred or intolerance of other social groups, especially on the basis of race or sexuality.")[2]

The matter is more complicated than simply saying that the U.S. Constitution protects hate speech and many schools regulate it, however. Not all hateful speech is protected speech, even under the First Amendment, which allows for certain restrictions on hate speech. For instance, harassment—whether based on gender or race—can rise to the level of restricted speech, as can words that incite violence. This "fighting words" doctrine remains controversial—many free expression advocates consider it bad law—but it is still the law of the land in the United States.

***

On a Saturday afternoon in April 1940 in Rochester, New Hampshire, Walter Chaplinsky, a Jehovah's Witness, was distributing leaflets promoting his religion in a public place. A disturbance arose around Chaplinsky as townspeople objected to his reference to other religions as a "racket." James Bowering, a city marshal, arrived on the scene. Chaplinsky claimed he was punched by one or more members of an angry mob before being escorted to the police station for his protection. Bowering, representing the state, and Chaplinsky, seeking to spread the word about his religious beliefs, ended up in a dispute.

The altercation that ensued between Chaplinsky and Bowering gave rise to today's "fighting words" doctrine. Chaplinsky's words spoken to the marshal lay at the heart of the case before the Supreme Court. In the course of their interaction, Chaplinsky said to Bowering, the marshal: "You are a God-damned racketeer" and "a damned Fascist." Bowering, in turn, arrested Chaplinsky on the grounds of breaching the peace by uttering these words in this way. Chaplinsky admitted to saying these things, though he denied uttering the name of the deity.

Chaplinsky's case wound its way up to the U.S. Supreme Court. The dispute centered on whether the statute under which Chaplinsky was convicted—chapter 378, section 2, of the Public Laws of New Hampshire—passed muster under the Constitution. The statute read:

No person shall address any offensive, derisive or annoying word to any other person who is lawfully in any street or other public place, nor call him by any offensive or derisive name, nor make any noise or exclamation in his presence and hearing with intent to deride, offend or annoy him, or to prevent him from pursuing his lawful business or occupation.[3]

The Supreme Court unanimously held the statute to be permissible under the First Amendment. This case has been cited for decades as standing for the proposition that the state may lawfully prohibit "fighting words."[4]

The Supreme Court has further elucidated its opinion since the holding in *Chaplinsky*, which has long given rise to criticism from scholars.[5] In a 2003 case, *Virginia v. Black*, the court described fighting words as "those statements where the speaker means to communicate a serious expression of an intent to commit an act of unlawful violence to a particular individual or group of individuals."[6] The court interpreted "intimidation"—in the sense of expression not protected by the First Amendment—as a "type of true threat, where a speaker directs a threat to a person or group of persons with the intent of placing the victim in fear of bodily harm or death."[7] While the notion of a "true threat" might fail the Supreme Court's reasoning if tested again today, the "fighting words" doctrine remains good law in the United States.

I begin the discussion of hate speech with these key "fighting words" cases to draw attention to the fact that not all "hate speech" is protected speech, even under the U.S. Constitution. This subtlety is important in the context of assessing the degree to which campus administrators might restrict hate speech in a manner that is still in keeping with the First Amendment.

On campuses, administrators must navigate complicated legal waters when it comes to hateful speech. For instance, in Massachusetts, a state law requires educational institutions to regulate hazing, harassment, and bullying.[8] Gender and racial harassment, too, can violate both state and federal law. And in many places, administrators strive to meet another standard: ensuring that students benefit from an environment in which they can focus on learning, free from harassing speech. The hard question for administrators is how to strike an appropriate balance between protected speech that is necessary for a genuine exploration of ideas in the context of one's education and hate speech that diminishes students' ability to learn.

***

On campuses today, hate speech tops the list of the most intractable topics related to free speech and diversity. Hate speech cases are hard in large measure because they inevitably give rise to high emotion. Those who use hate speech often seek to press the limits of free expression purposely. Just as children test the limits that their parents set, those who express themselves through hateful words and actions are often testing the boundaries of what they can get away with.

This testing is not without consequence—particularly in the close confines of a learning community. The effects of hateful speech are often felt overwhelmingly by those in the minority on campuses. In other cases, hate speech targets female students and staff who may be in the majority on some campuses but who have historically been marginalized. Much of the time, those affected have done nothing to prompt the harmful speech—they are just minding their own business, trying to get an education. Hate speech is, at the very least, an unwanted distraction to the students, faculty, and staff at whom it is directed.

Hate speech can cause real psychological harm. The inequity of hateful speech being disproportionately borne by some members of society lies at the core of the argument made by social justice advocates that campuses should have stronger speech codes, including rules that curtail hateful speech. The sharpest limit of tolerance theory—and of strong free speech rights in the context of hate speech—is that most often the burden of tolerating hate falls unevenly on those who feel marginalized for one reason or another.

Laws oriented toward educational institutions often acknowledge this problem of disproportionate harm to marginalized individuals in a community. For instance, the Massachusetts statute that regulates hazing, harassment, and bullying notes:

Each [school antibullying] plan shall recognize that certain students may be more vulnerable to becoming a target of bullying or harassment based on actual or perceived differentiating characteristics, including race, color, religion, ancestry, national origin, sex, socioeconomic status, homelessness, academic status, gender identity or expression, physical appearance, pregnant or parenting status, sexual orientation, mental, physical, developmental or sensory disability or by association with a person who has or is perceived to have 1 or more of these characteristics. The plan shall include the specific steps that each school district, charter school, non-public school, approved private day or residential school and collaborative school shall take to support vulnerable students and to provide all students with the skills, knowledge and strategies needed to prevent or respond to bullying or harassment.[9]

While this statute focuses on environments for school-age children, it makes plain an important concept. The burden of bearing hateful speech tends to fall disproportionately on those in the minority on campuses of all types.

One of many reasons to take the long view on the topic of free expression is that the dynamic of who is in the minority is likely to change. Those who find themselves in the majority at one moment may be in the minority at another, and vice versa. In nineteenth-century Boston, for instance, the dominant Protestant community regularly discriminated against Catholic immigrants from Ireland. The infamous sign "No Irish need apply" that hung in Boston shop windows stood for a deep-seated, pernicious discrimination against the Irish. But by the late twentieth century, the Irish Catholic community had become the undisputed powerhouse of Boston politics. Once the butt of harsh criticism and hate speech, many Boston Irish (among other Caucasians living in Boston at the time) paid the hate forward during the dispute over school integration and the busing of students in the 1970s. The residents of South Boston—some of them descendants of those who had been discriminated against in the nineteenth century—in turn expressed virulent racism against the African-American community in the late twentieth century. The point is not that Boston's Protestants or Irish Catholics have been, or are today, any more racist than anyone else. The point is simply that those who are on one end of discrimination are wise to recall that they may be on the other end at another point in history.

Those arguing for stronger speech codes during the Obama administration may be thinking twice about calling for speech restrictions on campuses in a United States led by President Trump. If the machinery of censorship were to limit the use of the term *racist* or *privileged* with respect to white men or to curb criticism of symbols such as state or national flags, the dynamic involved would take on a different cast. Principles that protect speech and call for equity serve everyone, not just the ascendant or the marginalized at any given moment.

The proliferation of hate speech online is another reason to reconsider the way a campus handles this type of expression.[10] The online environment is rife with hateful speech of every variety, available from anywhere through the powerful mobile devices carried around in students' pockets and pulled out in nearly any free moment. The growth of hate speech online, in communities around the world as well as on our campuses, connects the harms that our students face locally with the harms that others experience globally. While no one has a good solution to the problem of the cross-border flow of hateful speech and its effects, the reality of these changed circumstances needs to be factored into any campus-based calculation. What happens locally can reverberate online, connecting with similar occurrences elsewhere, in ways that can be consequential.

At any given historical moment, there are strong reasons to allow wide latitude for political opinions on campus to protect both free expression and academic integrity, when many schools also value diversity, equity, and inclusion in just as fundamental a way. What is to be done when these values clash in a digitally networked era?

***

As educators, we ought to begin by making clear to students that we consider hateful speech, on campuses and otherwise, abhorrent. One of the purposes of education can be, and should be, to teach tolerance and empathy, which in turn ought to diminish the utterance of hateful speech on campuses and beyond. This starting point is just as important as the starting point in favor of broad discretion for speech on campuses. Educators should also give voice, unequivocally, to our obligation to ensure an environment in which all students can focus on their learning. That obligation extends not just to face-to-face encounters but to those online as well.

Campus administrators are right to listen to the claims of current students, who make us aware that hateful speech still happens on our campuses and that the effects of this speech can be deleterious to a learning environment. Often, these student activists argue that a particular conception of free speech is less important than the values of equity and inclusion on a campus. It is this clash of values that gives rise to the toughest moments: when a commitment to a genuinely diverse community comes up against an equally genuine commitment to a free and open environment for expression. The job of educators should be to ensure both values can thrive on campus to the greatest extent possible.

Administrators often create teams that address bigotry through programming and support. Arizona State University, for instance, has a long history of supporting this type of initiative, while also earning high marks for its commitment to free expression from FIRE and other observers. Today, some of this important work is conducted through its Committee for Campus Inclusion (CCI). As its webpage states, "Actions constitute harassment, if they substantially interfere with another's educational or employment opportunities, peaceful enjoyment of residence, physical security, and they are taken with a general intent to engage in the actions and with the knowledge that the actions are likely to substantially interfere with a protected interest identified in the subsection above. Such intent and knowledge may be inferred from all the circumstances."[11] Concurrently, the CCI webpage notes: "Neither this nor any other university policy is violated by actions that amount to expression protected by the state or federal constitutions or by related principles of academic freedom. This limitation is further described in the 'ASU First Amendment Guidelines,' the current version of which supplements this policy."[12] ASU purposefully sets out to honor both diversity and free expression through its campus inclusion work.

Our starting point as educators should be with efforts to prevent hate speech in the first place, while also making clear the importance of ensuring that political views of all persuasions, respectfully shared, have a place on campus. A goal of universities should be to eliminate hate speech, even as some degree of noxious expression must be tolerated by all sides in any debate. To the extent that prevention doesn't work, a school should do what it can to mitigate the effects on those targeted. This work should happen in classrooms, in orientations, and in plenary meetings of the community. Academic communities that fail to work on teaching tolerance up front are likely to experience the ill effects of conflict as students test out their ideas in insensitive ways.

***

Despite our best efforts to prevent it, hateful speech arises on campuses just as it does in the world at large. There is no easy answer to how to handle hate speech on campuses when it arises—or when it seeps onto a campus from afar, via social media. If a university adopts the First Amendment as its guide, the range of permissible speech is not unlimited but is relatively wide. To limit the effect of hate speech through other means, that university might commit to a renewed emphasis on programming and support for the legitimate concerns of those affected, just as

ASU did. If a community chooses to add a campus speech code instead, the answer will always end up being case by case. Institutions that do adopt speech codes must address the critique that their implementation may curtail academic freedom and the learning that is the primary point of university life.[13]

A school's educational mission should drive its policymaking. Context matters enormously in terms of how a learning community handles clashes between claims related to free expression and the desire to clamp down on hateful speech.

This range of approaches on campuses establishes a form of pluralism that in itself is a good thing. FIRE conducts an annual survey of campus speech codes, providing an important guide to students and administrators regarding the range of policies.[14] Major universities with a strong free expression tradition, such as the University of Chicago, are right to make plain their philosophy to prospective scholars and students alike.[15] Columbia University, under the leadership of First Amendment scholar Lee Bollinger, makes clear to its students that it, too, will follow the principles of the First Amendment on campus.[16] State universities and those funded directly by the government may not have a choice: they are commonly deemed to be "state actors" that must uphold the First Amendment protections.[17]

Even for a state school, it is possible to craft campus policies, including disciplinary codes, that are devoted to balancing free expression with tolerance for a broad range of students and faiths. Schools and universities often disallow speech that amounts to gender or racial harassment; intimidating other students through phone calls or online messaging; or inciting violence against other students. Schools also strike this balance by distinguishing between speech and conduct—a blurry and sometimes unhelpful line, but one that is often invoked.[18] Speech that is directed toward an individual and interferes with their ability to engage in the educational program can and should be treated as a disciplinary matter. No student should be able to harass another student. These rules can be, and often are, crafted in such a way that they are consistent with the First Amendment.

In a legal sense, private schools and religious institutions have more room to maneuver than state schools, should they wish to restrict speech further than the First Amendment would permit. A religious school, driven in its decision making by a different mission, might adopt a different set of speech rules than a secular institution. A private high school, with younger students and a mission to develop strong character as well as a spirit of inclusion, likewise might decide to impose tighter limits on permissible speech than a major public university would.

As critical as I was in chapter 2 of the ham-handed letter from the University of Chicago dean at the start of the 2016 school year, the policy of the university at large is laudable, especially insofar as it is consistent with, and tied directly to, the university's long-standing goals. As the University of Chicago stated in its recent *Report of the Committee on Freedom of Expression*, "From its very founding, the University of Chicago has dedicated itself to the preservation and celebration of the freedom of expression as an essential element of the University's culture."[19] The University of Chicago places freedom of expression at the center of its set of values and makes that commitment clear to students and faculty from the outset. No student or faculty member joining the community could reasonably mistake the university's policy for anything other than full-throated support for free expression.

The hard questions tend to arise when a private school decides to impose a speech restriction to curtail hate speech that would not be permissible under the First Amendment. My view is that a private school certainly may invoke restrictions that are more protective of campus minorities than the First Amendment would permit. That is especially true in the context of K–12 schools where the stage of development of the learners is different in meaningful ways from the stage of development of university students. It is also plausible that private colleges and universities may adopt a set of rules deviating from the requirements of the First Amendment.

A student attending a private school with a different history and a different mission than, say, the University of Chicago, might reasonably expect that the institution would adopt a different posture when hate speech arises. For instance, a school founded in the Catholic tradition might adopt practices in line with the teachings of that faith. A Jewish university, likewise, might sensibly adopt rules distinct from the rules set by the Constitution. A historically black college or university (HBCU), established for the purpose of educating young people of African or African-American descent, might adopt yet another set of rules that favor certain forms of inclusion over its commitment to free expression in certain cases. A women's college might make choices based on the commitment to single-sex education that lies near the heart of its mission. Private institutions should be admired when they clearly state their values and then carry them out with fidelity even when conflicts arise.

As critics from FIRE and elsewhere rightly contend, the main concern when it comes to the speech restrictions of private institutions is duplicity. If a private school says one thing about its commitment to free expression and then does something else, the school has misled incoming students. Many of the speech codes that arose in the 1980s and 1990s ran afoul of this concern. As FIRE establishes on its website:

Private colleges and universities are contractually bound to respect the promises they make to students. Many institutions promise freedom of expression in university promotional materials and student conduct policies, but then deliver selective censorship once the first tuition check is cashed. They may not be bound by the First Amendment, but private institutions are still legally obligated to provide what they promise. Private institutions may not engage in fraud or breach of contract.

It is important to note, however, that if a private college wishes to place a particular set of moral, philosophical, or religious teachings above a commitment to free expression, it has every right to do so. The freedom to associate voluntarily with others around common goals or beliefs is an integral part of a pluralistic and free society. If a private university states clearly and publicly that it values other commitments more highly than freedom of expression, that institution has considerably more leeway in imposing its views on students, who have given their informed consent by choosing to attend.[20]

The best approach for administrators is to establish clear expectations for students on campus. Where a college, university, or school expects that it might restrict speech more than the First Amendment would allow, it should say so, and it should act accordingly when its values come into conflict. The number of institutions that do so effectively, according to FIRE's reporting, is very low. Only 6 percent (27) of the 449 schools reviewed by FIRE in its 2017 Spotlight report earned a "green light," up from 22 in the previous year's report.[21]

Arizona State University is not the only institution that appears to be balancing these interests effectively. According to FIRE, the "green light" institutions include several others that have also enacted significant diversity-related policies. Duke

University and Purdue University, for instance, have strong policies on bias, hate speech, and peaceable assembly on their books
along with strong support for free expression. Policies are necessary but not sufficient; getting it right in practice can often be far
harder than striking a balance on paper. But sound policies are
nonetheless a crucial step in the process toward strong, inclusive
communities that also value free expression.

***

When might it be appropriate for a private school or university to restrict hate speech more than the First Amendment
would allow? Recall, again, that the First Amendment allows for
a degree of restriction of hate speech—that which falls under
the "fighting words" doctrine or that which constitutes gender
or racial harassment, for instance. Imagine, though, that the
speech involved does not meet the strict requirements of today's
Supreme Court doctrine when it comes to hate speech. When
could the school or university reasonably intervene in the interest of protecting minorities, or any target of hate speech, in a
campus environment?

Suppose, for example, that a group espousing hatred—say,
the KKK or a neo-Nazi group—were to begin a march on the
grounds of a private college or university campus in the middle
of a school day. The same march in the town square two miles
away would be frowned on by the locals but it would be hard, if
not impossible, for the government to shut it down under the
First Amendment. The famous case involving the neo-Nazi group
that sought to demonstrate publicly in the town of Skokie, Illinois, established the First Amendment protection for such hateful expression.[22] Would a school administrator be within his or
her rights to call campus security to force the marchers to leave
the campus?

In my view, the answer is plainly yes, especially if the school had been clear up front about its values and policies, and established that its commitment to a diverse, equitable, and inclusive campus is on a par with its commitment to free expression. In this show of hate speech on the campus green, in front of the students who have freely assembled together in the school community, the neo-Nazi marchers would be acting in a manner inconsistent with the values of the school. The right to free expression of the marchers is not greater than the right of the campus community members to a learning environment free of this sort of hate. The balance points exactly the other way: the intrusion of this hateful speech exceeds the value of permitting this particular form of speech in the campus community.

This example demonstrates the extent to which there is a reasonable limit as to how and when a campus community must practice tolerance. While certain political speech—even obnoxious speech—must be permitted on campuses in order to pursue the truth and to allow free and open debate, there must be a limit to the degree of hatefulness of the speech that the community should allow.

The paradox of tolerance lies at the heart of this example. Must the tolerant always tolerate the intolerant?

***

We teach more than just mathematics, science, writing and reading, languages, the arts, and other academic topics in our schools. We also teach character and moral development. Many schools do so explicitly, through the lessons that we choose; all schools do so implicitly, through the personal examples that faculty members, coaches, administrators, and staff set for our students. Whether parents like it or not, there is no way for teachers to avoid teaching character to some extent; after all, our students watch us as they learn.

At the core of this character development, we ought to teach tolerance. But tolerance can be an extremely tricky value to convey when it comes down to it. Never in recent memory has it been trickier than in the wake of the 2016 presidential election.

It is extremely easy to be a tolerant person when everyone around you is tolerant. It is easy to tolerate the tolerant. It is easy to teach the tolerant. If everyone in a learning community commits to this principle, things go well. Schools should aim for a community in which everyone commits to a deep, abiding sense of tolerance. That would make matters much more straightforward—in this respect, anyway.

The problem with tolerance is when it comes to the intolerant. To the extent that some people in society are intolerant of other people—and we know that to be true—there becomes, all of a sudden, a problem with tolerance. The tolerant are called on to tolerate the intolerant. Meanwhile, the intolerant, in turn, are not asked to tolerate anyone.

To some degree, in a democracy, we must tolerate intolerance; that is part of the deal. We do not just give votes to the tolerant. It is also true that we grow and learn when we tolerate the views of others with whom we disagree. As Lee Bollinger argued in *The Tolerant Society*, a community, and individuals, grow stronger through the extraordinary self-control of tolerating harmful speech.

But the idea of tolerance must also have its limits. The philosopher Karl Popper, writing in 1945, defined this "paradox of tolerance": "Unlimited tolerance must lead to the disappearance of tolerance. If we extend unlimited tolerance even to those who are intolerant, if we are not prepared to defend a tolerant society against the onslaught of the intolerant, then the tolerant will be destroyed, and tolerance with them." In this famous passage, Popper went a great deal further in exploring when intolerant political philosophies should be suppressed:

In this formulation, I do not imply, for instance, that we should always suppress the utterance of intolerant philosophies; as long as we can counter them by rational argument and keep them in check by public opinion, suppression would certainly be unwise. But we should claim the right to suppress them if necessary even by force; for it may easily turn out that they are not prepared to meet us on the level of rational argument, but begin by denouncing all argument; they may forbid their followers to listen to rational argument, because it is deceptive, and teach them to answer arguments by the use of their fists or pistols. We should therefore claim, in the name of tolerance, the right not to tolerate the intolerant. We should claim that any movement preaching intolerance places itself outside the law, and we should consider incitement to intolerance and persecution as criminal, in the same way as we should consider incitement to murder, or to kidnapping, or to the revival of the slave trade, as criminal.[23]

Popper went too far in this powerful statement, but the essence of his point still rings true today. One need not extend the argument so far as he does—say, to the criminalization of incitement to intolerance (with which I do not agree)—to grasp the rationale for a degree of liberal intolerance. Writing these words in Europe at the end of World War II, Popper had good reason to wish there had been an earlier restriction of intolerance.

There is no reason why a private campus should be required to play host to a group that espouses racial or ethnic hatred that is counter to a core value of the institution. Even if that same speech would be permitted in the city square, an administration that allows it to disrupt an otherwise functional learning environment does more harm than good. It may be that a democracy will come to a point at which it can tolerate all forms of hateful speech in all its educational institutions, but I do not believe that we are at that point today. The disruptive psychological toll of the most extreme, hateful speech is too high a price for members of marginalized groups on campuses to be expected to pay—especially during this period of steady diversification and growing, but incomplete, equity and inclusion on campuses.

Though the law almost certainly says otherwise today, I believe that even public colleges and universities ought to be able to reach the same decision when it comes to keeping the most hateful speech—of the sort embodied, say, in a KKK or neo-Nazi rally—off campus. The value in terms of teaching and learning of this sort of expression in the context of an academic community does not compensate for the distraction and harm caused to students. The fact that the harm and the distraction would fall disproportionately on a subset of students should factor into the analysis by educators. If schools are in fact about ensuring that a diverse group of young people have a place to learn, administrators should be able to choose whether the most hateful forms of speech have a place on campus. A specific statute or a new Supreme Court holding might be required to make such campus rules possible at a state university. While those who believe that free speech is more important than diversity might disagree, a conversation about line drawing at the edges of permissible speech on campus is well worth having.

Even as we all must tolerate views we hate up to a point in a democracy, there must also be a point at which the tolerant are allowed to be intolerant of those who are intolerant. Our study of history points to examples when it was a terrible mistake to tolerate intolerance for too long. This paradox of tolerance is much on our minds today, once again, as we seek a way forward after a wrenching election season in 2016. As schools and as a democracy at large, we need to determine where the line falls between hateful speech that we must tolerate and intolerant speech that we must resist.

The 2016 election has given rise to hard conversations on this point. What made that election so painful for many people was that too much of the rhetoric was about exclusion, not inclusion; it was about hate, not about love; it was about elevating some people above others. The winning presidential candidate, Donald Trump, espoused hatred during his campaign toward Mexicans and Muslims in particular—and as president immediately moved to put restrictive policies in place toward both groups. During the campaign, Trump failed to denounce hate groups that target underrepresented people of color. He mocked the disabled on national television. He demonstrated a misogynist streak that made members of his own party denounce his candidacy in large numbers—and led to one of history's largest demonstration, in dozens of cities, the day after his inauguration. The rhetoric during the campaign, from all sides, emphasized division and supremacy of some over others, not equity and inclusion. It is also a fact that this patently divisive approach to running for president resulted in his victory in the Electoral College, if not in the popular vote. We are a divided nation, separated from one another in some fundamental way. The 2016 election cycle was structured around this divide.

These facts are not presented in a manner meant to be partisan. The problem is not about Democrats and Republicans. It is about the values that we hold as educational institutions and how to honor them as we teach our young people. Many of the views expressed during the 2016 campaign are inconsistent with the kinds of values that many, if not virtually all, of our schools stand for—the kinds of values, including tolerance, that we seek to teach.

In our schools, we value and support all our students and their well-being equally. That must include those who are Muslim and Mexican, and those who come from all faiths and all racial and ethnic backgrounds. That must include conservatives as well as liberals. In our classrooms, those on the right must tolerate those on the left; those on the left must tolerate those on the right. No one should be bullied or otherwise mistreated because of who they are or who they or their parents voted for. Serious political discussion must have a place in our academic communities as well as in society at large. Students need to have equal support when it comes to their learning and growth, no matter their perspective or background. (The expectation of equality and inclusion is not limited to our school environments. Recall that we are expected to value and support all people equally in society at large, too, in the plain language of our Declaration of Independence and our Constitution.)

Hateful speech, targeting individuals and groups on our campuses, is not serious political discussion; it should have no place in our schools. In the hyped-up context of campus and electoral events between 2014 and 2017, we must be vigilant for the way our students interpret political events and their lessons. We must focus on where the line should fall between the political speech that we must tolerate and the hateful speech that we should not.

As an educator, I believe we must do everything we can to focus on building tolerance and respect for one another so we do not find ourselves, as school communities, faced with this paradox repeatedly. As a citizen, I believe the same is true for the United States at large. We ought to make extensive room for the conversations we need to have about politics and difference. But intolerance of one another on our campuses, and in our communities, is something that we ought to find ways to prevent and to resist.

***

No speech code or disciplinary handbook—no matter how carefully drafted—can anticipate every controversy, especially of this sort. The approach of educational leaders should be to state clearly the values of the institution; to teach tolerance and limit hateful speech in the first place; to teach about the values of free expression and the free exchange of ideas as a general matter; to be clear with students and adults up front about how disputes will be handled; and to ensure that the ensuing debates are as open and constructive as possible. Despite these best efforts, the most complicated acts of expression by those wishing to push the boundaries will prompt case-by-case analysis. Just as they do in the courts, these cases will always give rise to strong emotions and heated debates.[24]

For a democracy comprised of diverse constituents to work, everyone must be tolerant of others to a very large degree. Both those liberals and those conservatives who espouse tolerance of others' views as a key virtue must be prepared to tolerate a great deal of speech with which they disagree. Serious philosophical disagreement must be able to take place on campuses or the intellectual enterprise is lost.

Our system of governance must also allow for a point at which the tolerant may become intolerant of intolerance. The intolerant should not be able to dominate merely by calling on the tolerant to tolerate their intolerance. The hard problem of hate speech is where that line—between the political speech we must tolerate, no matter how obnoxious, and the hate speech we should not tolerate—is drawn. Educational communities may have to struggle through more hard cases, not fewer, as campuses become more heterogeneous. Some campuses are plainly getting more adept than others at managing this heterogeneity. A full-throated commitment to both diversity and free expression, interdependent and mutually supporting, should preface, and then carry through, each instance of that struggle.

6   Free Press and Freedom of Assembly

The First Amendment sets forth not just one but five freedoms: the right to free expression, a free press, free exercise of religion, freedom of peaceful assembly, and the right to seek redress from the government. Two of these freedoms are rarely at issue in the present-day conversations related to diversity and free expression on campuses: the right to appeal to the government for redress of grievances is literally not relevant; the right to the free exercise of religion comes up from time to time, but is not a central matter in these discussions. (That is not to say that religious freedom is not essential, nor to say that it is not under threat in various ways; the point is simply that it is not customarily connected to this larger set of concerns.) Though not the main focus of this short book, two of the other freedoms enumerated in the First Amendment are deeply connected to the current debate over free expression and diversity: the right to a free press and the right to peaceful assembly.

***

At a systemic level, democracies rely on a free and independent press as an essential institution. A free press serves many purposes, chief among them providing a check on powerful state actors and ensuring the opportunity for citizens to become informed and engaged in civic life. A free press means also that any individual or group can publish their views as openly as any other individual or group. That freedom does not guarantee that every press outlet will reach an equally large audience, nor does it mean that money, power, and legacy are irrelevant in terms of the reach of media outlets. Political candidates, for instance, commonly complain that the news media are "biased"—today, according to many U.S. citizens, the media are allegedly biased in terms of supporting candidates and causes on the left side of the political spectrum.[1] History is filled with such claims, favoring one group or another. What a constitutional right to a free press does mean is that the system, in theory, gives everyone an equal opportunity to participate in public discourse.

On campuses, the right to a free press plays an important role in conjunction with the right to free expression. There are two ways in which a free press relates directly to the debate on free expression and diversity. First, student publications play an important role in mediating discourse on campuses. Some campuses have free and independent news organizations; others allow for administrators to affect what runs in publications. Second, campuses often serve as the site of debates over whether the administrators ought to permit outside news media to cover events occurring on campus—itself an important and contested matter.

Campus news organizations play an essential role in both agenda setting and discussion of the salient news in an academic community. Most commonly, these organizations take the form of student newspapers. They also include radio stations, weekly news magazines, and other types of publications. Virtually all campuses have one or more types of news organizations run by students for the purpose of covering news in and relevant to the community.

Campus news organizations support democracy by providing an active, hands-on laboratory in which students engage in the craft of journalism. The more they can learn about and share in the true experience of journalism in the larger world, the better. Democracies need well-trained journalists to function properly and schools ought to provide these training grounds for interested students.

These news organizations also play an essential role in mediating the conversations that take place on campuses. A well-run campus news organization, led by responsible student journalists, helps to establish a fact base that can ground conversations in a constructive way. As in a city or town, a newspaper of record provides an outlet for multiple voices to reach an audience of interested fellow citizens. A campus news organization might also editorialize in ways that help to draw attention to key issues and, occasionally, to shape policy by decision makers such as administrators and trustees. The campus newspaper might also provide a constructive outlet for student opinion on the op ed page.

As an academic administrator, I am well aware that an uncensored and independent campus news organization can drive adults on campus crazy, especially when students make mistakes in judgment or reporting (sometimes both at the same time). Despite this tendency, these organizations have a crucial function. The trade-off between a free and independent campus news organization, inevitably fallible, and a news organization that answers to campus administrators is often hotly debated on campuses. From a First Amendment and free expression perspective, the choice in favor of a free and independent campus press is clear.

The case against a free, independent campus news organization can be made in several ways. The strongest case is that student journalists are not yet trained in their craft. When empowered to operate an uncensored news organization, students are granted awesome power before they have the skill to exercise it responsibly. When they make mistakes, whether of fact or judgment, there are real casualties—the pain suffered by an individual or family, or the distortion of the truth. Even the students themselves, years later, might wish that they had not been granted such power and latitude so early in their lives. The existence of the Internet exacerbates that concern: a student journalist's mistake in digital form could haunt them for the rest of their lives, whereas a print journalist's errors are more quickly forgotten. We used to wrap fish in yesterday's newspapers; no fish are wrapped in the digital versions of a reporter's stories.

The best answer to that critique is not censorship but rather teaching, support, training, and a sound editorial structure. The school has a responsibility to ensure that the student journalists have access to the guidance they need in order to be able to exercise the power they wield. That support can take the form of faculty and alumni with expertise in journalism passing down their knowledge to students, as well as funding for training in the craft of reporting. The school can also hold out the threat of revoking the institutional charter for the news organization to operate, to the extent that it violates the conventions of sound journalism.

The costs of a censored or administratively controlled campus news environment are very high. Consider the effects of a system in which the university president can tell student reporters not to run a story critical of a particular presidential candidate. According to news reports, that is exactly what happened in 2016 at Liberty University, a private, Christian university based in Lynchburg, Virginia. Joel Schmieg, the sports editor of the *Liberty Champion*, the university's student newspaper, says that he was told by the university president, Jerry Falwell Jr., not to run a column critical of presidential candidate Donald Trump. The irony of the president of a school called "Liberty University" clamping down on the freedom of the press on his own campus was not lost on the news media. A second irony: the purportedly negative column about candidate Trump reached a much larger audience than it would ever have when the alleged censorship was publicized in national media outlets such as the *Daily Beast* and directly on the student's Facebook page.[2]

***

The right of the press to cover campus protests is likewise tied into the conversations about free expression and diversity. Here, one might sensibly distinguish between two types of press coverage: coverage by campus journalists, who are typically enrolled students, and coverage by the outside press, which may wish to report on campus events for an audience beyond the college or university. An example of the second scenario—in which the national press seeks to cover campus protests—has attracted national attention in recent years.

An altercation at a student protest on the University of Missouri campus in November 2015 brought the right to a free press into sharp relief. A group of students associated with the group Concerned Student 1950 sought to create a "safe space" on campus for their protest against racist incidents that had marred their campus for years—use of racist language against African-American students and faculty, the appearance of cotton balls across public campus spaces to invoke plantation slavery, feces placed in the shape of a swastika, and other hateful speech directed toward minority groups. A press photographer, Tim Tai, sought access to the space occupied by the protestors in order to take pictures. A heated altercation between Tai and the protestors led to national discourse about the respective interests of the press to cover on-campus activities and the interests of the students not to be covered by outside press during a protest.[3]

Additional facts associated with this incident complicate the narrative. Tai was both a student on the campus—a senior student of photojournalism at the University of Missouri School of Journalism—and a freelancer taking pictures for ESPN. Tai was therefore both an "insider" and an "outsider." In today's media environment, a photograph taken on a campus, especially one published by a major national news outlet, would potentially be seen by millions of people and almost certainly would persist online for a very long time, if not for the life of the students involved. In a video published online, two adults affiliated with the university appear to side with the student activists in seeking to bar Tai from photographing the group. Both Tai and the students who were protesting had legitimate concerns that they sought to vindicate in the altercation.[4]

In the aggregate, U.S. college students support the notion of a free press, but they also see some of the complexities involved in cases such as Tai's at the University of Missouri. In a recent Knight Foundation poll, 70 percent of college students believed that students should not be able to prevent the press from covering protests on college campuses (as compared to 76 percent of U.S. adults). This overall sentiment suggests that a strong majority of today's college students, and adults, would favor Tai's interests in the Missouri case.

At a more nuanced level, however, students were divided when prompted to evaluate certain potential reasons for curtailing press access. Nearly half of U.S. college students agreed that there are sometimes legitimate reasons to curtail outside press access to student protests on campus. When the reason was that people at the protest or public gathering believed reporters would be biased, 49 percent thought that curtailing press access would be appropriate. When the people at the protest said they have a right to be left alone, 48 percent said they believed that curtailing access would be appropriate. When presented with the reasons that the people at the protest want to tell their own story on the Internet and social media, 44 percent thought it would be appropriate to curtail press access.[5] This deeper split in perceptions demonstrates that many students appreciated the concerns of the protesters in the case involving Tai on the University of Missouri campus.

A free press on campuses serves important functions, both locally within the community and in terms of training journalists for a life of important service in a democracy. There are costs associated with a free press on campuses, however. Students do make reporting mistakes, just as adult journalists do, and they can be painful, especially when amplified by social media. Student protestors have raised important points about the limits of press freedom in certain spaces and contexts. The debate as to what constitutes appropriate time, place, and manner restrictions on press freedom—as an analogy to its close cousin, the right to free expression—will continue to arise over time.

No one clear rule can govern well in all these instances. Rather, we will continue to balance a series of legitimate interests in search of a balance between liberty and equality. The case involving Tai on the Missouri campus helps to show the complexity often involved in these competing claims. The right to press freedom serves society at large and ought to be protected. There are, however, times and places when people do have a right to be left alone; there must be limits to where the press can intrude in day-to-day life. These disputes can only be managed by a process approach over time in which we assess and balance the legitimate interests of all parties involved.

***

Since the ratification of the First Amendment, the right to peaceful assembly has worked in concert with the right to free expression and the right to a free press to ensure equitable ability to spread and to hear a message. Much like the right to free expression and a free press, the right to peaceful assembly is strong but not absolute. This right prohibits the federal government from passing a law that would block most forms of peaceful assembly. As in the case of free speech, the government can insist on time, place, and manner restrictions, with a comparable series of balancing tests to determine whether the restrictions are appropriate. The same set of protections for individuals have been extended to the states via the Fourteenth Amendment.[6]

The right to peaceful assembly has played an essential role throughout U.S. history to ensure that people can come together in public, regardless of their political viewpoints and without harassment from the state. Unlike the right to free expression or the right to a free press, the right to peaceful assembly has not given rise to high-profile disputes on campuses in recent years. However, the status of this right is on the minds of many students, probably because of other highly publicized public gatherings that have been curtailed by the police.

According to a recent Gallup survey commissioned by the Knight Foundation and the Newseum, race is a major factor in the perception of First Amendment rights among college students. The difference is stark: non-Hispanic black college students are much less likely than non-Hispanic white college students to believe the right of people to assemble peacefully is secure, at 39 percent vs. 70 percent, respectively. To put it differently, fewer than half of non-Hispanic black college students believe the right to assemble peacefully is secure, whereas a significant majority of non-Hispanic white college students believe that right is secure.[7]

The timing of this survey in 2016, amid the many protests related to police violence against African Americans, offers a possible explanation for this large difference. During this period, many of the campus activists brought the national race discourse to campus. In doing so, many of these students were at least carefully tracking, if not directly involved in, off-campus protests around the United States, in Ferguson, Missouri, and Baltimore, Maryland, among other places. In many of these instances, students saw footage of violent confrontations with police officers charged with keeping the peace at the protests. Tensions were running high in many cities and on campuses as well.

Taken together, these recent survey findings demonstrate that most students do support First Amendment protections, but they also recognize some of the tensions involved. The survey findings also reveal that students' perception of how secure these rights are varies dramatically based on their racial background. This troubling divide points to the need for open dialogue about the importance of these rights, as well as about the reasons behind the students' widely held concerns.

The struggle for civil rights in the United States has long been integrally linked to the debate over civil liberties, such as free expression, a free press, and the freedom of peaceful assembly. As members of academic communities and democracies, we must listen with care to one another's perspectives, recognizing in particular that there are racial, class, and other divides in how certain freedoms are perceived. We should strive to implement policies that accomplish all of these essential goals at once. Though frequently in tension, these goals have long proved compatible. On our campuses in particular, they can and ought to be.

7 Why the Diversity and Free Expression Debate Matters

In the fall of 2016, while doing research for this book about free expression and diversity, I took a short break from my steady diet of serious nonfiction. As engaged as I was with the topic at hand, I welcomed the prospect of escape that fiction offers from all else that consumes us. Reviews of British author Ian McEwan's new book, *Nutshell*, tempted me to drop everything and read it as soon as I could get a copy.

It turned out that I wasn't escaping the topic after all. Near the end of the novel, McEwan pulled me back into the reality of the moment and the political disputes on our campuses. The story in *Nutshell*—roughly, a "whodunit"—is narrated by an about-to-be-born child. I won't say any more that might spoil the plot other than to quote a passage, told from the child's perspective, looking ahead to his education:

A strange mood has seized the almost-educated young. They're on the march, angry at times, but mostly needful, longing for authority's blessing, its validation of their chosen *identities*. The decline of the West in new guise perhaps. Or the exaltation and liberation of the self. A social-media site famously proposes seventy-one gender options—netrois, two-spirit, bigender ... any colour you like, Mr. Ford. Biology is not destiny after all, and there's cause for celebration. ... If my identity is that of a believer, I'm easily wounded, my flesh torn to bleeding by any questioning of my faith. Offended, I enter a state of grace. Should inconvenient opinions hover near me like fallen angels or evil djinn (a mile being too near), I'll be in need of the special campus safe room equipped with Play-Doh and looped footage of gambolling puppies. Ah, the intellectual life! I may need advance warning if upsetting books or ideas threaten my very being by coming too close, breathing on my face, my brain, like unwholesome dogs.[1]

As a satirist of today's students, McEwan has a lot of company. Newspaper columnists, think tank analysts, television pundits— they all have taken shots at the easy mark of college students and administrators as we adjust to a changing educational landscape. The satirists abound in part because, too often, they have plenty to take aim at. Student activists can certainly avoid making themselves such an easy mark; it is true that the overreach is a common feature of campus debates led by earnest, enthusiastic undergraduates. As academic administrators know from experience, too often student activists undermine their own good causes when they take aim at people who are in fact their allies in the larger scheme of things or seek redress on issues that are well beside the point.

Snarky critiques of student activists distract from the underlying issues that are in fact fundamental, issues that run to the deep-seated racial and class tensions in the United States and much of Western Europe today. As communities become more diverse than ever before—in cities and on campuses alike—we will need, repeatedly, to work out the tension between diversity, equity, and inclusion on the one hand and free expression on the other. The increasing interconnection between online and offline conversations means that these debates will continue to grow in their reach and importance. The outcome of what appear to some to be frivolous debates is in fact consequential.

Communities will be strongest if we can find a sound resolution—neither in the form of a facile synthesis nor a one-sided rout, but rather in the form of a sustainable pathway forward. The health of our educational institutions and our democracies depends on it.

***

Democracy cannot succeed unless those who express their choice are prepared to choose wisely. The real safeguard of democracy, therefore, is education.

—President Franklin Delano Roosevelt[2]

Free expression is part and parcel of the way students gain the laudable educational benefits of diversity in a campus community; diversity is part and parcel of how students gain the benefits of an open, challenging educational environment. It is through this connection, and through the citizens we teach in our schools, that education can lead to a stronger democracy.

The tolerance theory of free expression, proposed by legal scholar and university president Lee Bollinger and examined at several points in this book, makes plain this connection. A primary rationale for free expression derives from its propensity to increase tolerance in individuals and communities. The tolerance theory holds that the act of forgiving those who express hurtful views develops empathy and strength in those who forgive. And young people benefit from being able to express their views freely—up to a point—regardless of whether they perceive adults to be expounding a "right answer."

The educational imperative to focus on a positive learning environment should guide the way a school or university handles the most difficult speech-related cases that are sure to arise. There are, of course, limits to the speech that can be permitted—even under the tolerance theory and even for those state universities and others that follow the First Amendment as their guide. Other communities may choose to draw the lines around impermissible speech more sharply. A grade school community, for instance, might establish tighter limits on expression than a high school, which in turn should have tighter limits than a university. As among private universities, there is bound to be a range of approaches, depending on the institutions' goals. The essential point that joins these varied approaches is that the values of free expression and tolerance for the views and backgrounds of others in education transcend the requirements of law.

A degree of pluralism in the educational approaches of schools and universities is a good thing. Rather than decrying this form of diversity, we would do better to embrace it. Schools make plain to prospective students their approach to education through the way they handle issues of free expression and diversity. While my personal preference as a student happens to have been to study in a large university setting that takes the First Amendment as a guide and that also emphasizes a strong equity and inclusion program, others may choose to attend another type of college with a different emphasis. The University of Chicago has staked out its position very clearly; others do so through their communications and their policies. This diversity in approaches within higher education, and in private schools at all levels of learning, is a strength of our system of academic freedom.

Students from all political stripes can benefit from learning in a campus environment in which their teachers and invited guests are free to express a broad range of viewpoints. Many schools and universities, so capable in teaching the liberal arts

in all their breadth, are not doing so well in presenting a heterogeneity of political viewpoints on campus. While there are various reasons for the left-leaning tilt to many faculties and for the
prevalence of far-right views on others, this absence of serious
and diverse views on campuses can do our students a disservice.
A range of viewpoints among the faculty and staff as well as
among the students leads to a stronger academic environment,
just as it does in a democracy at large. Without this heterogeneity, it is hard to argue that our campuses are in fact devoted to
free inquiry.[3]

The absence of a heterogeneity of viewpoints on our campuses is both cause and symptom of the culture wars that have
been dividing our academic and political communities. Campuses that in fact do limit the range of political discourse enable
those who wish to politicize diversity to pit it against free expression. As forcefully as I believe that free expression and equity
and inclusion are not only compatible but interconnected, it is
also plain to me that campus environments can chill speech on
both the left and the right—expression that is a long way from
hate speech—in ways that are counterproductive. It would be a
mistake to graduate a generation of students who feel that they
cannot express political opinions in their schools and universities for fear of reprisals. We must resist any impulses that lead in
this direction.

Those on both sides of the political spectrum stand to gain
from a combination of diverse backgrounds, diverse views, and
a robust right to free expression. The Free Speech Movement of
the 1960s at Berkeley was led by the far left, ensuring that their
voices would be heard in protest against the conservative mainstream of the day. Today, Colin Kaepernick, the star quarterback
for the San Francisco 49ers, can refuse to stand for the National

Anthem or to salute the American flag precisely because the right to free expression allows him to do so.[4] As upset as they are by his message, those who challenge Kaepernick's right to express himself in this clear way are both failing to hear his message and failing to honor the flag that they profess to support so unstintingly. Outsiders of all political stripes throughout U.S. history have relied on the right to free expression to ensure that they may be heard.

Those all along the political spectrum should also honor, in equal measure, a commitment to diverse, equitable, and inclusive communities. On campuses, all students stand to benefit from a diverse array of peers—especially when we turn our various forms of diversity into community and individual strengths. The Supreme Court, likewise, based its decisions with respect to affirmative action—in the *Fisher*, *Grutter*, and *Gratz* cases—on the educational benefits of diversity. These cases also highlight the distinction between establishing laudable goals and enacting the practices that help students realize these educational benefits.[5] Every academic community should strive for a positive campus climate for teaching and learning, one in which building and promoting tolerance is a key goal. Students, in turn, gain essential skills—skills that they will need just as much as the substantive knowledge gained in their courses—to cope with a rapidly changing world.

Finally, everyone involved in the debate about free expression and diversity would benefit from a greater degree of listening to and empathy for others with a different political viewpoint. For those who claim there has been a "decline" in free expression rights, there is merit in stopping and listening more closely to the underlying concerns raised by campus activists, studying the data collected about youth attitudes to free expression, and seeking to help address them rather than satirizing them. For my own part, I have heard from campus activists that we have a long way to go in terms of creating truly equitable and inclusive learning environments, even in schools that have relatively strong track records on diversity in admissions. On the flip side, campus activists who wish to quell the views of others with whom they disagree would do well to listen more and to recall that the same speech restrictions used to stifle views of opponents today could be flipped easily in the future. The cost of chilling speech on campus, whether by the left or the right, is a real danger to the proper functioning of a school, university, or state. Genuine, shared values of tolerance, respect, and empathy in a community can ensure that free expression and diversity both thrive on campuses and in the world at large.

***

These campus debates are consequential on several levels. Although the context in schools is different than the context of our public squares, academic communities are microcosms of the societies in which they are embedded. Getting it right in the intentional community of a campus can be instructive in getting it right in the growing "cosmopolis," as Timothy Garton Ash calls it.[6] Our campuses are the places where many of our young people come of age and learn to act as citizens in their own right—an essential part of their education. The lessons we learn together on our campuses can help point the way toward living civilly and harmoniously in diverse communities. These debates are not, as the satirists might have us all think, frivolous academic squabbling; they are serious political disputes with long-term consequences.

Our students graduate into a world in the midst of unprecedented, seismic changes. As they enter adulthood and the workforce, they face a fast-changing workplace and culture, due to massive globalization combined with unheard-of demographic shifts. As economies spread and technologies improve, and our appetite for growth markets continues unabated, the world is becoming more and more interconnected. At the same time, political disputes are frequently fractured and polarizing—in 2016 alone, witness Brexit in the United Kingdom, the national referendum in Colombia, and the divisive presidential election in the United States. Put one way, our students are growing up in a world in which, in the words of critic Jeff Chang, "the energies of anxious whites have been diverted from class uprising toward racial division" due to the efforts of a string of candidates "from Wallace and Nixon to Palin and Trump."[7] Put another way, the racial and economic divides in our democracies are growing rather than shrinking, in frightening ways.

The potential for interconnection among people through technology is increasing just as these racial and economic divides are growing. At the advent of the Internet era, many hoped that the Internet would be a great boon for democracy, a space in which unfettered speech would lead to better decision making, greater transparency in government, and less corruption. While there have been gains in these areas in some respects, the use of the Internet and social media has instead often tended to have a less positive effect on democracies: increased divisiveness along political and other lines. The effect of hateful speech has grown when the conversation takes place online, reaching more people and often in harsher tones, egging individuals on to sharper and sharper positions. The vexing problem of the spread of "fake news" within and across online communities stems from similar dynamics. One of the main reasons why this tension between free speech and diversity is so important to resolve today is the interconnection between digital and offline communities and what it means for the functioning of democracies.

The importance of social media in our shared public lives is growing with time. Many of the acute disputes on our campuses, one way or another, involve online media in concert with face-to-face interactions. Young people on campuses use popular applications, such as Yik Yak, on which anonymous and hateful messages spread quickly. Applications that often involve real names are popular too: from Snapchat to Facebook, Instagram to Tumblr to who-knows-what tomorrow. These online communications spill over into classrooms and public forums on campuses, sometimes chilling speech or adding to the tension around sensitive issues. Students who learn to act as responsibly—and to make their case as forcefully—online as they do in face-to-face environments will be poised to thrive in the communities they join when they graduate. It is our job as their educators to teach these lessons in supportive environments while they are in our care.

Perhaps the most immediate and seismic of these shifts is demographic. If current trends continue, the United States will become a "minority majority" country by 2044.[8] This phenomenon mirrors trends in many other liberal democracies, playing out globally as well as at the city, state, and regional levels. It is most easily seen in the demographic shifts in incredibly diverse cities such as Toronto, Berlin, and Miami. As the composition of our communities becomes more and more diverse, our schools and universities seek to admit qualified students of all backgrounds, regardless of their ability to pay, their race, or their religion. These changes make the coexistence of a strong commitment both to equity and liberty an urgent matter.

Why? We ought to find a way to balance these two goals in order to ensure that everyone invited into an educational community feels welcomed, that everyone belongs, and that everyone has an equal opportunity to thrive in the community. That is the clear message that student activists have brought to campus after campus in recent years. These activists have demanded that both adults and young people of all sorts on campuses do better at this work of equity and inclusion, and they are right. Diversity itself is just about numbers; it is not a goal in itself. Equity and inclusion are the goals with meaning. Social science research shows that students who do not have a sense of belonging in a school community tend to perform less well. The same seems to be true about "performance" in the economy at large: those who feel engaged in a community and welcomed are more likely to contribute to the well-being of the whole. That is a major reason the United States feels so divided after the election of 2016 and why the United Kingdom feels so divided after the Brexit vote earlier that year. The absence of inclusion affects most underrepresented people of color and it affects poor, middle-aged whites in rural areas; these absences can become yawning divisions on campuses and in democracies alike. The process of becoming a diverse community and then achieving equity and inclusion for all is long and arduous. It requires hard work over an extended period of time by everyone in the community, not just those who perceive themselves to be at the margins for one reason or another.

We should honor the experience of every student because the act of doing so is itself a skill—a form of excellence—that every student should have by the time they graduate from school or university. This skill should be seen as part of a liberal arts education in the twenty-first century. Today's students need to learn how to live in a society where difference is the norm, not the exception. This skill—to be able to work and live across multiple lines of difference, to make it a blessing and not a curse, to find ways that it strengthens democracies, not undercuts them—is one that will serve students for the rest of their life. Parents and students alike should seek out those diverse communities that make this sort of learning and growth possible for our youth. It will serve individuals, economies, and political systems extremely well.

The rationale for free expression and the rationale for diversity are more alike than they are different. Freedom of speech, like diversity, provides legitimacy for the exercise of power. They both promote an informed, engaged public. They both help to establish the set of rules necessary for an equitable distribution of power in a democracy. These principles make democracy work more effectively and more equitably.

In the long run, no one stands to benefit from pitting these ideals against one another, as convenient as it may seem for political purposes in a heated moment, in the midst of a culture war. Too often, those who wish to silence protesters point to free speech as being threatened. Instead, we ought to acknowledge the reality in the vast majority of these examples: for campus activists, these acts represent free speech being *used*, not resisted.[9] And campus activists ought to ensure that their speech is not crowding out the legitimate political speech of others.

An essential part of the work of education is to prepare young people for lives of active citizenship. The role of an engaged citizen in a highly diverse, interconnected culture is different today than it once was. As educators and as students, we need to work at growing our empathy and compassion for one another. We should work toward preserving and honoring our cultural differences, while avoiding a form of color blindness that pretends that no differences in experience exist across race, class, gender, faith, and other dimensions of identity. As we do so, we must preserve a strong form of intellectual freedom in which discourse and disagreement on important topics are not just tolerated but encouraged. With seriousness of purpose and respect for one another, there is no reason that free expression and diversity cannot and should not coexist on our campuses and in increasingly diverse communities at large—enriching the lives of all students and all citizens along the way.

In setting educational policies today, our focus must be on the long run. Those of us who set these policies ought to engage our communities in collective problem-solving when tension arises on campuses. We should set sensible ground rules that ensure that community members feel included and encouraged to participate broadly. If we are to save our planet, create new jobs, reduce world hunger, mitigate the effects of conflict and war, and improve healthcare for those in every society, our students will need to hone the skill of working across differences—solving hard problems while also being able to disagree. This skill is necessary to develop in our young people if democracy is to work at any scale, much less at a global scale. We need to prepare graduates who will thrive as citizens, producers, and leaders in a world of increasing diversity, complexity, and connectedness. We need to teach explicitly the way that free expression benefits all people in a society and how the First Amendment works in practice—often best learned through shared experience in solving problems together. The hard work of teaching and learning these types of skills needs to be happening on all of our campuses and to extend to the world beyond the campus walls.

Since well before the founding of the United States, liberty and equality have been in tension. The debate about free expression and diversity is today's manifestation of that long-running tension. Historically, we have done a better job at ensuring liberty for some than for others. Strong feelings about that inequity have given rise to many of the campus protests we have witnessed—or been a part of—in the last few years. As we look to the future, our goal ought to be to have liberty and equality, free expression and diversity, in more or less equal measure for all citizens. This goal is not easily achieved, especially given the passions involved. As educators, we hold the potential to bring about this bright future in our hands every day. We must not squander it.

Notes

Chapter 1

1. "Black Lives Matter" website, http://blacklivesmatter.com.

2. "African American Policy Forum #SayHerName" website, http://www.aapf.org/sayhername.

3. "The Demands" website, http://www.thedemands.org.

4. Alex Garcia, "Why Diversity in Media Matters in Making Free Speech Really Free," *Medium*, https://medium.com/@Alex_Garcia/why-diversity -in-media-matters-in-making-free-speech-really-free-a25cb760bd80# .zay4kev7j.

5. "Saddam Wins '100% of Vote,'" *BBC News*, October 16, 2002, http://news.bbc.co.uk/2/hi/2331951.stm.

6. University of Chicago Office of LGBTQ Student Life Safe Space website, https://lgbtq.uchicago.edu/page/safe-space.

7. For an alternative view, see Arao and Clemens, "From Safe Spaces to Brave Spaces."

Chapter 2

1. Scott Jaschik, "U Chicago to Freshmen: Don't Expect Safe Spaces," *Inside Higher Ed*, August 25, 2016, https://www.insidehighered.com/

news/2016/08/25/u-chicago-warns-incoming-students-not-expect-safe
-spaces-or-trigger-warnings.

2. Roger Pilon, "The University of Chicago Has No Room for Crybullies," *Cato at Liberty* (blog), August 25, 2016, http://www.cato.org/blog/
university-chicago-has-no-room-crybullies.

3. Jay Michaelson, "University of Chicago's P.C. Crackdown Is Really
about Keeping Right-Wing Donors Happy, *The Daily Beast*, August 26,
2016, http://www.thedailybeast.com/articles/2016/08/26/university-of
-chicago-s-p-c-crackdown-is-really-about-keeping-right-wing-donors
-happy.html.

4. Scott Jaschik, "The Chicago Letter and Its Aftermath," *Inside Higher
Ed*, August 29, 2016, https://www.insidehighered.com/news/2016/08/
29/u-chicago-letter-new-students-safe-spaces-sets-intense-debate.

5. Angus Johnston, "A Map of American Student Activism 2014–15,"
Student Activism (blog), December 2, 2014, https://studentactivism
.net/2014/12/02/a-map-of-american-student-activism-2014-15.

6. Susan Svrluga, "U. Missouri President, Chancellor Resign over Handling of Racial Incidents," *Washington Post*, November 9, 2015, https://
www.washingtonpost.com/news/grade-point/wp/2015/11/09/missouris
-student-government-calls-for-university-presidents-removal.

7. "Yale Launches Five-Year, $50 Million Initiative to Increase Faculty
Diversity," Yale University website, November 3, 2015, http://news
.yale.edu/2015/11/03/yale-launches-five-year-50-million-initiative
-increase-faculty-diversity; Conor Friedersdorf, "Brown University's
$100 Million Inclusivity Plan," *The Atlantic*, November 24, 2015, http://
www.theatlantic.com/politics/archive/2015/11/brown-universitys-100
-million-plan-to-be-more-inclusive/416886.

8. Patrick Maines, "Campus Protests and Blatant Attacks on Free
Speech," *The Hill* (blog), November 25, 2015, http://thehill.com/blogs/
pundits-blog/education/261259-campus-protests-and-blatant-attacks
-on-free-speech.

9. Greg Lukianoff and Jonathan Haidt, "The Coddling of the American Mind," *The Atlantic*, September 2015, http://www.theatlantic.com/magazine/archive/2015/09/the-coddling-of-the-american-mind/399356.

10. "History of Hillel," Hillel International, http://www.hillel.org/about/hillel-story.

11. "The Safe Space Ally Network," LGBTQ Student Life, University of Chicago, https://lgbtq.uchicago.edu/directories/table/safe-space-ally-network.

12. Alex Morey, "U. Chicago's 'Academic Freedom' Letter a Win for Campus Speech [Updated], FIRE (Foundation for Individual Rights in Education) website, August 25, 2016, https://www.thefire.org/u-chicagos-academic-freedom-letter-a-win-for-campus-speech/.

13. Beth McMurtrie, "One University Asks: How Do You Promote Free Speech without Alienating Students?," *Chronicle of Higher Education*, October 23, 2016, http://www.chronicle.com/article/One-University-Asks-How-Do/238146/.

14. "The Colliding of the American Mind," *The Economist* website, June 4, 2016, http://www.economist.com/news/international/21699905-university-protesters-believe-they-are-fighting-justice-their-critics-think-free.

15. Alexander, *New Jim Crow* (see especially chapter 3, "The Color of Justice," for references to numerous studies demonstrating the differential rates of incarceration among races in the United State); Kennedy, *Race, Crime, and the Law*; Stevenson, *Just Mercy*

16. *Chronicle of Higher Education, The Almanac of Higher Education 2016–17* (Washington, DC: Chronicle of Higher Education, 2016), http://www.chronicle.com.ezp-prod1.hul.harvard.edu/interactives/almanac-2016.

17. Ibid.

18. National Center for Educational Statistics, "Race/Ethnicity of College Faculty: Fast Facts," https://nces.ed.gov/fastfacts/display.asp?id=61.

19. Guinier, *Tyranny of the Meritocracy*.

20. "The Quiet Discrimination of Microinequities: A Q&A with Adjunct Professor Mary Rowe," MIT Sloan website, February 3, 2016, http://mitsloan.mit.edu/newsroom/articles/the-quiet-discrimination-of-microinequities-a-qa-with-adjunct-professor-mary-rowe/.

21. Steele, *Whistling Vivaldi.*

22. Adam K. Raymond, "The Alleged Offenses of 2014's Disinvited Commencement Speakers," *New York Magazine* website, May 15, 2014, http://nymag.com/daily/intelligencer/2014/05/disinvited-graduation-speakers-alleged-offenses.html.

23. Ask a Librarian, Harvard Law School Library, "What Are the Origins of the Harvard Law School Shield That Was Retired in 2016?," http://asklib.law.harvard.edu/faq/115307.

24. "Harvard Corporation Agrees to Retire HLS Shield," *Harvard Law Today*, March 14, 2016, http://today.law.harvard.edu/harvard-corporation-agrees-to-retire-hls-shield.

25. Annette Gordon-Reed and Annie Rittgers, "A Different View," March 2016, https://today.law.harvard.edu/wp-content/uploads/2016/03/Shield_Committee-Different_View.pdf.

26. John Fabian Witt, Chair, et al., Yale University, "Letter of the Committee to Establish Principles on Renaming," http://president.yale.edu/sites/default/files/files/CEPR_FINAL_12-2-16.pdf.

27. Yussef Robinson, "Oxford's Cecil Rhodes Statue Must Fall—It Stands in the Way of Inclusivity," *The Guardian*, January 19, 2016, https://www.theguardian.com/commentisfree/2016/jan/19/rhodes-fall-oxford-university-inclusivity-black-students.

28. Gabriel Fisher, "Princeton and the Fight over Woodrow Wilson's Legacy," *New Yorker*, November 25, 2015, http://www.newyorker.com/news/news-desk/princeton-and-the-fight-over-woodrow-wilsons-legacy.

29. Jesse Singal, "Why the University of Chicago's Anti–'Safe Space' Letter Is Important," *New York Magazine* website, August 26, 2016, http://nymag.com/daily/intelligencer/2016/08/the-university-of-chicagos-anti-safe-space-letter-matters.html.

30. Dautrich, *Future of the First Amendment* (2004, 2011, 2014, 2016); Dautrich and Yalof, *Future of the First Amendment* (2006, 2007); Dautrich, Yalof, and López, *Future of the First Amendment* 2008.

31. *Free Speech on Campus*, Knight Foundation website, April 4, 2016, http://www.knightfoundation.org/reports/free-speech-campus.

32. *National Undergraduate Study*, sponsored by the William F. Buckley, Jr. Program at Yale and conducted by McLaughlin & Associates, October 26, 2015, posted online at https://www.dropbox.com/s/sfmpoeytvqc3cl2/NATL%20College%2010-25-15%20Presentation.pdf?dl=0.

33. Howard Gillman and Erwin Chemerinsky, "Don't Mock or Ignore Students' Lack of Support for Free Speech. Teach Them," *Los Angeles Times*, March 31, 2016, http://www.latimes.com/opinion/op-ed/la-oe-chemerinsky-gillman-free-speech-on-campus-20160331-story.html.

34. "Free Speech on Campus."

35. For ideas, see, e.g., Haynes et al., *The First Amendment in Schools*.

Chapter 3

1. Amy Howe, "Finally! The *Fisher* decision in Plain English," *SCOTUS* (blog), June 24, 2013, http://www.scotusblog.com/2013/06/finally-the-fisher-decision-in-plain-english.

2. Chicago-Kent College of Law at Illinois Tech, "*Fisher v. University of Texas*," Oyez website, https://www.oyez.org/cases/2012/11-345.

3. *Brown v. Board of Education of Topeka*, Opinion, May 17, 1954; Records of the Supreme Court of the United States, Record Group 267, National Archives.

4. Chicago-Kent College of Law at Illinois Tech, "*Grutter v. Bollinger*," Oyez website, https://www.oyez.org/cases/2002/02-241; Chicago-Kent College of Law at Illinois Tech, "*Gratz v. Bollinger*," Oyez website, https://www.oyez.org/cases/2002/02-516.

5. Banaji and Greenwald, *Blindspot*.

6. Steele, *Whistling Vivaldi*.

7. Ibid., 6.

8. Kennedy, *Race, Crime, and the Law*; Alexander, *New Jim Crow*; Stevenson, *Just Mercy*.

9. Martha Minow, *In Brown's Wake: Legacies of America's Educational Landmark* (Oxford: Oxford University Press, 2010), 158–159.

10. Alicia Garza, "A Herstory of the #BlackLivesMatter Movement by Alicia Garza," FeministWire.com, October 7, 2014, http://www.thefeministwire.com/2014/10/blacklivesmatter-2.

11. Giovanni Russonello, "Most Americans Hold Grim View of Race Relations, Poll Finds," *New York Times*, July 13, 2016, http://www.nytimes.com/2016/07/14/us/most-americans-hold-grim-view-of-race-relations-poll-finds.html.

12. Pew Research Center, "On Views of Race and Inequality, Blacks and Whites Are Worlds Apart," June 27, 2016, http://www.pewsocialtrends.org/2016/06/27/on-views-of-race-and-inequality-blacks-and-whites-are-worlds-apart.

13. Page, *Diversity and Complexity*, 6.

14. Fisher v. University of Texas, 579 U.S. ____ (2016), 16.

15. Mina Huang, "Diversity Matters: The Beauty and Power of Difference," *Pearson Higher Education Blog*, June 19, 2015, http://www.pearsoned.com/education-blog/diversity-matters-the-beauty-and-power-of-difference.

16. Thomas Jefferson, "The Declaration of Independence," National Archives ed., 1776, http://www.archives.gov/exhibits/charters/declaration_transcript.html.

17. Ta-Nehisi Coates, "The Case for Reparations," *The Atlantic*, June 2014, http://www.theatlantic.com/magazine/archive/2014/06/the-case-for-reparations/361631.

18. Pettigrew and Tropp, "Intergroup Contact"; Goldsmith, "Shaping Race Relations"; Sidanius, *Diversity Challenge*.

19. Jeremy C. Fox, "Babson College Student Appears to Apologize for Wellesley Incident," *Boston Globe*, November 13, 2016, https://www.bostonglobe.com/metro/2016/11/12/babson-student-apologizes-for-wellesley-incident/DfB9lp4Ec30BO6KIqXz35I/story.html.

20. William Frey, "Diversity Defines the Millennial Generation," *The Avenue*, Brookings Institution, June 28, 2016, http://www.brookings.edu/blogs/the-avenue/posts/2016/06/28-diversity-millennial-frey.

21. William Frey, "New Projections Point to a Majority Minority Nation by 2044," *The Avenue*, Brookings Institution, December 12, 2014, http://www.brookings.edu/blogs/the-avenue/posts/2014/12/12-majority-minority-nation-2044-frey.

22. Pew Research Center, "10 Demographic Trends That Are Shaping the U.S. and the World," March 31, 2016, http://www.pewresearch.org/fact-tank/2016/03/31/10-demographic-trends-that-are-shaping-the-u-s-and-the-world.

23. Fisher v. University of Texas, 579 U.S. ____ (2016), 16, originally in the University of Texas at Austin's submissions to the Court at Supp. App. 23A.

Chapter 4

1 Abrams v. United States, 250 U.S. 616 (1919).

2. Ibid. The cases the Supreme Court Justices had in mind included *Schenck v. United States*, 249 U.S. 47 (1919), and *Frohwerk v. United States*, 249 U.S. 204 (1919). See also "*Abrams v. United States*" on the website of the Chicago-Kent College of Law, https://www.oyez.org/cases/1900-1940/250us616.

3. Ibid., 630–631.

4. Healy, *Great Dissent*.

5. Milton, *Areopagitica.*

6. Douglass, "Plea for Free Speech."

7. Erasmus, *Education of a Christian Prince.*

8. U.S. Const. amend. I.

9. Marsh v. Alabama, 326 U.S. 501 (1946); Pruneyard Shopping Center v. Robins, 447 U.S. 74 (1980).

10. Fish, *There's No Such Thing.*

11. Stone, *Perilous Times*, 8.

12. Bollinger, *Tolerant Society.* For a critique of Bollinger's General Tolerance Theory, see Paul Brest, "How Free Do We Want to Be?," *New York Times*, June 8, 1986, http://www.nytimes.com/1986/06/08/books/how-free-do-we-want-to-be.html.

13. Douglass, "Plea for Free Speech."

14. William Lloyd Garrison to William James Potter, Oct. 11, 1873, call no. Ms.A.1.1 v.8, p.30B, Boston Public Library.

15. Ruth Tenzer Feldman and Bettina Aptheker, "The Free Speech Movement: 50th Anniversary," *Kidlit Celebrates Women's History Month* (blog), March 24, 2014, http://kidlitwhm.blogspot.com/2014/03/the-free-speech-movement-50th.html.

16. John Perry Barlow, "Declaration of Independence of Cyberspace," Electronic Frontier Foundation, 1996, https://www.eff.org/cyberspace-independence.

17. Ibid.

18. Ryan Girdusky, "New Anti-Hillary Hashtag Shows Bernie Supporters Aren't Going Quietly," Red Alert Politics website, May 24, 2016, http://redalertpolitics.com/2016/05/24/new-anti-hillary-hashtag-shows-bernie-supporters-arent-going-quietly.

19. Janell Ross, "What an Anti-Hillary Hashtag Tells Us about Sexism in the 2016 Campaign," *Washington Post,* January 26, 2016, https://www

.washingtonpost.com/news/the-fix/wp/2016/01/26/wordthatmightdesc
ribetheamericanvoter.

20. Bird, Taylor, and Kraft, "Student Conduct," 183–205.

Chapter 5

1. "Spotlight on Speech Codes 2017: The State of Free Speech on Our Nation's Campuses," FIRE's website, https://www.thefire.org/spotlight-on-speech-codes-2017.

2. *Oxford English Dictionary*, online entry for "hate speech," http://www.oed.com.ezp-prod1.hul.harvard.edu/view/Entry/84550?redirectedFrom=hate+speech#eid21206310.

3. Chaplinsky v. New Hampshire, 315 U.S. 568 (1942). The *Chaplinsky* opinion may be accessed in a reliable form online at Cornell's Legal Information Institute website, https://www.law.cornell.edu/supremecourt/text/315/568.

4. *Chaplinsky* itself deserves much more discussion on several fronts. Some legal scholars believe the decision should be overturned. See Caine, "Trouble with 'Fighting Words,'" 443–562, http://scholarship.law.marquette.edu/cgi/viewcontent.cgi?article=1026&context=mulr. Others find the *Chaplinsky* opinion problematic insofar as the Court's decision focused on the statute and not on what Chaplinsky said to the marshal. The words Chaplinsky used are political speech that would almost certainly enjoy First Amendment protection if tested on their merits today. It is hard to imagine that what Chaplinsky did would in fact have incited violence against the marshal; from what we know of the facts, it is much more likely that he was the one at risk of harm, not so much the government official. For further discussion, see also FIRE's website for an analysis of *Chaplinsky* and other Supreme Court decisions relevant to campus speech at https://www.thefire.org/misconceptions-about-the-fighting-words-exception.

5. David L. Hudson Jr., "'Fighting Words' Case Still Making Waves on 70th Anniversary," the First Amendment Center website at

Vanderbilt University and the Newseum, March 9, 2012, http://www
.firstamendmentcenter.org/fighting-words-case-still-making-waves-on
-70th-anniversary.

6. Virginia v. Black, 538 U.S. 343, 359 (2003).

7. Ibid., 360.

8. Mass. Gen. Laws ch. 71, § 37O (2016).

9. Mass. Gen. Laws ch. 71, § 37O(d)(3) (2016).

10. Faris et al., "Harmful Speech Online."

11. See "Policy Statement Supporting Diversity and Free Speech" on
the website of the Office of the University Provost at Arizona State
University, https://provost.asu.edu/committees/cci/policies.

12. Ibid.

13. Greg Lukianoff and Jonathan Haidt, "The Coddling of the American
Mind," *The Atlantic*, September 2015, http://www.theatlantic.com/
magazine/archive/2015/09/the-coddling-of-the-american-mind/
399356; Lukianoff and Haidt, *Coddling of the American Mind*.

14. FIRE, "Spotlight on Speech Codes 2017."

15. University of Chicago, Office of the Provost, *Report of the Committee
on Freedom of Expression*, January 2015, https://provost.uchicago.edu/
sites/default/files/documents/reports/FOECommitteeReport.pdf.

16. Columbia University, Office of Communications and Public Affairs
website, "President Lee C. Bollinger's 2016 Convocation Address:
Learning from Freedom of Expression," August 29, 2016, http://news
.columbia.edu/content/1272.

17. Kermit L. Hall, "Free Speech on Public College Campuses
Overview," the First Amendment Center website at Vanderbilt
University and the Newseum, September 13, 2002, http://www
.firstamendmentcenter.org/free-speech-on-public-college-campuses. See
also "Free Speech, Public Universities, and State Actors as First Amend-

ment Speakers," *PrawfsBlawg* (blog), February 10, 2006, http://prawfsblawg.blogs.com/prawfsblawg/2006/02/free_speech_pub.html.

18. Schauer, "Between Speech and Action."

19. University of Chicago, *Report of the Committee on Freedom of Expression.*

20. "Private Universities," FIRE website, https://www.thefire.org/spotlight/public-and-private-universities/.

21. FIRE, "Spotlight on Speech Codes 2017."

22. Geoffrey Stone, "Remembering the Nazis in Skokie," *Huffington Post*, May 20, 2009, http://www.huffingtonpost.com/geoffrey-r-stone/remembering-the-nazis-in_b_188739.html. See also *National Socialist Party of America v. Village of Skokie*, 432 U.S. 43 (1977).

23. Popper, *Open Society*, 581.

24. For one side of the debate, framing some of the key issues involved, see "Hate Speech on Campus," American Civil Liberties Union (ACLU) website, https://www.aclu.org/other/hate-speech-campus.

Chapter 6

1. Noland D. McCaskill, "Poll: Majority of Voters Believe Media Biased against Trump," *Politico*, October 19, 2016, http://www.politico.com/story/2016/10/poll-media-bias-against-donald-trump-229998.

2. Ben Collins, "Student: Jerry Falwell Jr. Axed Anti-Trump Story from Liberty University's School Newspaper," *Daily Beast*, October 10, 2016, http://www.thedailybeast.com/articles/2016/10/18/jerry-falwell-axes-anti-trump-story-from-liberty-university-s-student-newspaper.html.

3. Terrell Jermaine Starr, "There's a Good Reason Protesters at the University of Missouri Didn't Want the Media around," *Washington Post*, November 11, 2015, https://www.washingtonpost.com/posteverything/wp/2015/11/11/theres-a-good-reason-protesters-at-the-university-of-missouri-didnt-want-the-media-around/?utm_term=.6a6b107c0ec3.

See also the press release from the School of Journalism at University of Missouri, "Dean David Kurpius Comments on Student's Coverage of Protest on Carnahan Quad," November 10, 2016, https://journalism .missouri.edu/2015/11/dean-david-kurpius-comments-on-students -coverage-of-protest-on-carnahan-quad; Krishnadev Calamur, "What's Happening at the University of Missouri?," *The Atlantic*, November 9, 2015, http://www.theatlantic.com/national/archive/2015/11/whats -happening-at-the-university-of-missouri/414870.

4. Austin Huguelet and Daniel Victor, "'I Need Some Muscle': Missouri Activists Block Journalists," *New York Times*, November 9, 2015, http:// www.nytimes.com/2015/11/10/us/university-missouri-protesters-block -journalists-press-freedom.html.

5. *Free Speech on Campus* (Miami: Knight Foundation, April 4, 2016), Knight Foundation website, http://www.knightfoundation.org/reports/ free-speech-campus.

6. See "Right to Peaceful Assembly: United States" on the Library of Congress website, last modified August 24, 2016, https://www.loc.gov/ law/help/peaceful-assembly/us.php.

7. *Free Speech on Campus*, Knight Foundation.

Chapter 7

1. McEwan, *Nutshell*.

2. Franklin D. Roosevelt, "Message for American Education Week," September 27, 1938, online by Gerhard Peters and John T. Woolley, The American Presidency Project, http://www.presidency.ucsb.edu/ws/?pid =15545.

3. Chris Sweeney, "How Liberal Professors Are Ruining College: In New England, They Outnumber Conservatives 28 to 1. Why That's Bad for Everyone," *Boston Magazine*, January 2017, http://www.bostonmagazine .com/news/article/2016/12/20/liberal-professors. See also "The Heterodox Academy" website, http://heterodoxacademy.org.

4. Steve Wyche, "Colin Kaepernick Explains Why He Sat during National Anthem," NFL website, August 27, 2016, http://www.nfl.com/ news/story/0ap3000000691077/article/colin-kaepernick-explains-why -he-sat-during-national-anthem.

5. Clarke and Antonio, "Rethinking Research."

6. Garton Ash, *Free Speech*.

7. Chang, *We Gon' Be Alright*.

8. William Frey, "New Projections Point to a Majority Minority Nation by 2044," *The Avenue*, Brookings Institution, December 12, 2014, http:// www.brookings.edu/blogs/the-avenue/posts/2014/12/12-majority -minority-nation-2044-frey.

9. Jelani Cobb, "Race and the Free Speech Diversion," *New Yorker*, November 10, 2015, http://www.newyorker.com/news/news-desk/race and the free speech diversion; Conor Friedersdorf, "Free Speech Is No Diversion," *The Atlantic*, November 12, 2015, http://www.theatlantic .com/politics/archive/2015/11/race-and-the-anti-free-speech-diversion/ 415254/.

Bibliography

Adams, Mike. "Academic Freedom on Trial: Adams v. UNCW and the Welcome Erosion of Garcetti." *Academic Questions* 28, no. 1 (2015): 54–65. doi:10.1007/s12129-015-9469-0.

Adams Family. *Adams Family Correspondence*. Eds. L. H. Butterfield, Wendell D. Garrett, and Marjorie E. Sprague. Cambridge, MA: Belknap Press / Harvard University Press, 1963.

Affolter, Jacob. "Fighting Discrimination with Discrimination: Public Universities and the Rights of Dissenting Students." *Ratio Juris* 26, no. 2 (2013): 235–261.

Alexander, Larry. *Is There a Right of Freedom of Expression?* Cambridge: Cambridge University Press, 2005.

Alexander, Michelle. *The New Jim Crow: Mass Incarceration in the Age of Colorblindness*. New York: New Press; distributed by Perseus Distribution, 2010.

Allport, Gordon W. *The Nature of Prejudice*. 25th anniversary ed. New York: Perseus, 1979.

Altman, Andrew. "Equality and Expression: The Radical Paradox." *Social Philosophy & Policy* 21, no. 2 (Summer 2004): 1–22.

Altman, Andrew. "Liberalism and Campus Hate Speech: A Philosophical Examination." *Ethics* 103, no. 2 (1993): 302–317.

Amdur, Robert. "Scanlon on Freedom of Expression." *Philosophy & Public Affairs* 9, no. 3 (1980): 287–300.

Amsden, Brian Scott. "Student Advocacy and the Limits of (Action-) Free Speech: Figurations of Materiality in Tinker, Bethel, and Hazelwood." *Communication and Critical/Cultural Studies* 8, no. 4 (2011): 353–375.

Arao, Brian, and Kristi Clemens. "From Safe Spaces to Brave Spaces." In *The Art of Effective Facilitation: Reflections from Social Justice Educators*, ed. L. M. Landreman, 135–150. Sterling, VA: Stylus Publishing, 2013.

Aristotle. *The Politics, and the Constitution of Athens*. Rev. ed. Ed. Stephen Everson. Cambridge: Cambridge University Press, 1996.

Badley, Graham. "A Place from Where to Speak: The University and Academic Freedom." *British Journal of Educational Studies* 57, no. 2 (2009): 146–163.

Bailey, Brigitte, Katheryn P. Viens, and Conrad Edick Wright, eds. *Margaret Fuller and Her Circles*. Durham: University of New Hampshire Press / University Press of New England, 2013.

Bailyn, Bernard. *The Ideological Origins of the American Revolution*. Cambridge, MA: Belknap Press of Harvard University Press, 1992.

Balkin, Jack M. "Free Speech Foundations Symposium: Cultural Democracy and the First Amendment." *Northwestern University Law Review* 110 (2016): 1053–1095.

Balkin, Jack M. "Free Speech and Press in the Digital Age: The Future of Free Expression in a Digital Age." *Pepperdine Law Review* 36 (2009): 427–444.

Banaji, Mahzarin R., and Anthony G. Greenwald. *Blindspot: Hidden Biases of Good People*. New York: Delacorte Press, 2013.

Barendt, E. M. *Freedom of Speech*. 2nd ed. New York: Oxford University Press, 2005.

Barnhardt, Cassie L. "Campus-Based Organizing: Tactical Repertoires of Contemporary Student Movements." *New Directions for Higher Education* 2014, no. 167 (2014): 43–58.

Barrow, Robin. "Academic Freedom: Its Nature, Extent and Value." *British Journal of Educational Studies* 57, no. 2 (2009): 178–190.

Batchis, Wayne. *The Right's First Amendment: The Politics of Free Speech & the Return of Conservative Libertarianism.* Palo Alto, CA: Stanford Law Books, 2016.

Bernstein, David E. *You Can't Say That! The Growing Threat to Civil Liberties from Antidiscrimination Laws.* Washington, DC: Cato Institute, 2003.

Bhagwat, Ashutosh. "Posner, Blackstone, and Prior Restraints on Speech." *Brigham Young University Law Review* 2015, no. 5 (2015): 1151–1181.

Bilgrami, Akeel. "Truth, Balance, and Freedom." *Social Research* 76, no. 2 (Summer 2009): 417–436.

Bilgrami, A., and J. R. Cole, eds. *Who's Afraid of Academic Freedom?* New York: Columbia University Press, 2015.

Bird, Lee E., Tawny Taylor, and Kevin M. Kraft. "Student Conduct in the Digital Age: When Does the First Amendment Protection End and Misconduct Begin?" In *Cutting-Edge Technologies in Higher Education,* Vol. 5: *Misbehavior Online in Higher Education,* ed. Laura A. Wankel and Charles Wankel, 183–205. Bingley, UK: Emerald Group Publishing, 2012.

Birney, Catherine N. *The Grimké Sisters: Sarah and Angelina Grimké.* Boston: Lee and Shepard, 1885.

Black, Donald J. *Moral Time.* New York: Oxford University Press, 2011.

Bok, Derek Curtis. *Beyond the Ivory Tower: Social Responsibilities of the Modern University.* Ed. Alfred D. Chandler. Cambridge, MA: Harvard University Press, 1982.

Bollinger, Lee C. *The Tolerant Society: Freedom of Speech and Extremist Speech in America.* New York: Oxford University Press, 1986.

Bollinger, Lee C., and Geoffrey R. Stone. *Eternally Vigilant: Free Speech in the Modern Era.* Chicago: University of Chicago Press, 2002.

Bowman, Nicholas A. "College Diversity Experiences and Cognitive Development: A Meta-Analysis." *Review of Educational Research* 80, no. 1 (2010): 4–33.

Bowman, Nicholas A. "Promoting Participation in a Diverse Democracy: A Meta-Analysis of College Diversity Experiences and Civic Engagement." *Review of Educational Research* 81, no. 1 (2011): 29–68.

Bowman, Nicholas A., and Julie J. Park. "Interracial Contact on College Campuses: Comparing and Contrasting Predictors of Cross-Racial Interaction and Interracial Friendship." *Journal of Higher Education* 85, no. 5 (2014): 660–690.

Boyd, Michelle J., Jonathan F. Zaff, Erin Phelps, Michelle B. Weiner, and Richard M. Lerner. "The Relationship between Adolescents' News Media Use and Civic Engagement: The Indirect Effect of Interpersonal Communication with Parents." *Journal of Adolescence* 34, no. 6 (2011): 1167–1179.

Broadhurst, Christopher J. "Campus Activism in the 21st Century: A Historical Framing." *New Directions for Higher Education* 2014 (167): 3–15.

Buckley, Phillip. "Subjects, Citizens, or Civic Learners? Judicial Conceptions of Childhood and the Speech Rights of American Public School Students." *Childhood* 21, no. 2 (May 2014): 226–241.

Butler, Johnnella E. "Replacing the Cracked Mirror: The Challenge for Diversity and Inclusion." *Diversity and Democracy* 17, no. 4 (Fall 2014), https://www.aacu.org/diversitydemocracy/2014/fall/butler.

Caine, Burton. "The Trouble with 'Fighting Words': Chaplinsky v. New Hampshire Is a Threat to First Amendment Values and Should Be Overruled." *Marquette Law Review* 88, no. 3 (Winter 2004): 441–562.

Campbell, Bradley, and Jason Manning. "Campus Culture Wars and the Sociology of Morality." *Comparative Sociology* 15, no. 2 (2016): 147–178.

Campbell, Bradley, and Jason Manning. "Microaggression and Moral Cultures." *Comparative Sociology* 13, no. 6 (2014): 692–726.

Campbell, David E., Meira Levinson, and Frederick M. Hess. *Making Civics Count: Citizenship Education for a New Generation*. Cambridge, MA: Harvard Education Press, 2012.

Campbell, Karlyn Kohrs. *Man Cannot Speak for Her*. New York: Greenwood Press, 1989.

Carlacio, Jami. "Ye Knew Your Duty, but Ye Did It Not": The Epistolary Rhetoric of Sarah Grimke." *Rhetoric Review* 21, no. 3 (2002): 247–263.

Center for Postsecondary Research, Indiana University School of Education. "National Survey of Student Engagement." August 10, 2016. http://nsse.indiana.edu/html/about.cfm.

Ceplair, Larry, Angelina Emily Grimké, and Sarah Moore Grimké. *The Public Years of Sarah and Angelina Grimké: Selected Writings, 1835–1839*. New York: Columbia University Press, 1989.

Chafee, Zechariah. *Free Speech in the United States*. Cambridge, MA: Harvard University Press, 1946.

Chang, Jeff. *We Gon' Be Alright: Notes on Race and Resegregation*. New York: Picador, 2016.

Chronicle of Higher Education. *The Almanac of Higher Education 2016–17*. Washington, DC: Chronicle of Higher Education, 2016.

Clarke, Chris Gonzalez, and Anthony Lising Antonio. "Rethinking Research on the Impact of Racial Diversity in Higher Education." *Review of Higher Education* 36, no. 1 (2012): 25–50.

Cohen-Almagor, Raphael. "Fighting Hate and Bigotry on the Internet." *Policy and Internet* 3, no. 3 (2011): 1–26.

Cohn, D'Vera, and Andrea Caumont. *10 Demographic Trends That Are Shaping the U.S. and the World*. Washington, DC: Pew Research Center, March 31, 2016. http://www.pewresearch.org/fact-tank/2016/03/31/10-demographic-trends-that-are-shaping-the-u-s-and-the-world/.

Cole, Jonathan R. *The Great American University: Its Rise to Preeminence, Its Indispensable National Role, Why It Must Be Protected*. New York: Public Affairs, 2009.

Curtis, Michael Kent. *Free Speech, "the People's Darling Privilege": Struggles for Freedom of Expression in American History*. Durham, NC: Duke University Press, 2000.

Darnton, Robert. *Censors at Work: How States Shaped Literature*. New York: Norton, 2014.

Dautrich, Kenneth. *Future of the First Amendment: Survey of High School Students and Teachers*. Commissioned by The John S. and James L. Knight Foundation. Miami: Knight Foundation, September 2004. http://www.knightfoundation.org/media/uploads/publication_pdfs/FOFA2004.pdf.

Dautrich, Kenneth. *Future of the First Amendment: Survey of High School Students and Teachers*. Commissioned by The John S. and James L. Knight Foundation. Miami: Knight Foundation, 2011. http://www.knightfoundation.org/media/uploads/publication_pdfs/Future-of-the-First-Amendment-full-cx2.pdf.

Dautrich, Kenneth. *Future of the First Amendment: Survey of High School Students and Teachers*. Commissioned by The John S. and James L. Knight Foundation. Miami: Knight Foundation, 2014. http://www.knightfoundation.org/future-first-amendment-survey.

Dautrich, Kenneth. *Future of the First Amendment: 2016 Survey of High School Students and Teachers*. Commissioned by The John S. and James L. Knight Foundation. Miami: Knight Foundation, 2017. https://knightfoundation.org/reports/future-of-the-first-amendment-2016-survey-of-high-school-students-and-teachers.

Dautrich, Kenneth, and David Yalof. *Future of the First Amendment: Survey of High School Students and Teachers*. Commissioned by The John S. and James L. Knight Foundation. Miami: Knight Foundation, September 2006. http://www.knightfoundation.org/media/uploads/publication_pdfs/survey_update2006.pdf.

Dautrich, Kenneth, and David Yalof. *Future of the First Amendment: Survey of High School Students and Teachers*. Commissioned by The John S. and James L. Knight Foundation. Miami: Knight Foundation, September 2007. https://s3.amazonaws.com/media.spl/559_fofa2007surveyo.pdf.

Dautrich, Kenneth, D. A. Yalof, and M. H. López, eds. *The Future of the First Amendment: The Digital Media, Civic Education, and Free Expression Rights in America's High Schools*. Lanham, MD: Rowman & Littlefield, 2008.

DeCew, JW. "Free Speech and Offensive Expression." *Social Philosophy & Policy* 21, no. 2 (Summer 2004): 81–103.

DelFattore, Joan. *Knowledge in the Making: Academic Freedom and Free Speech in America's Schools and Universities*. New Haven, CT: Yale University Press, 2010.

Denson, Nida, and Mitchell J. Chang. "Racial Diversity Matters: The Impact of Diversity-Related Student Engagement and Institutional Context." *American Educational Research Journal* 46, no. 2 (2009): 322–353.

DeSilver, Drew. *Young Adults: Less Trusting in General, but with Exceptions*. Washington, DC: Pew Research Center, May 23, 2013. http://www.pewresearch.org/fact-tank/2013/05/23/young-adults-less-trusting-in-general-but-with-exceptions/.

Douglass, Frederick. "A Plea for Free Speech in Boston." *Liberator*, December 14, 1860.

Downs, Donald Alexander. *Restoring Free Speech and Liberty on Campus*. Oakland, CA: Independent Institute / Cambridge: Cambridge University Press, 2005.

Dworkin, Ronald. *Freedom's Law: The Moral Reading of the American Constitution*. Cambridge, MA: Harvard University Press, 1996.

Dworkin, Ronald. "We Need a New Interpretation of Academic Freedom." Academic Freedom and the Future of the University Lecture Series. *Academe* 82, no. 3 (1996): 10–15.

Eagan, K., E. B. Stolzenberg, A. K. Bates, M. C. Aragon, M. R. Suchard, and C. Rios-Aguilar. *The American Freshman: National Norms Fall 2015*. Los Angeles: Higher Education Research Institute, UCLA, 2016.

Eagan, K., E. B. Stolzenberg, J. J. Ramirez, M. C. Aragon, M. R. Suchard, and C. Rios-Aguilar. *The American Freshman: Fifty-Year Trends, 1966–2015*.

Los Angeles: Higher Education Research Institute, UCLA, 2016. https://www.heri.ucla.edu/monographs/50YearTrendsMonograph2016.pdf.

Early, Gerald. "American Education and the Postmodernist Impulse." *American Quarterly* 45, no. 2 (1993): 220–229.

Early, Gerald. *Lure and Loathing: Essays on Race, Identity, and the Ambivalence of Assimilation*. New York: A. Lane / Penguin Press, 1993.

Early, Gerald. "The Quest for a Black Humanism." *Daedalus* 135, no. 2 (2006): 91–104.

Early, Gerald. "The Two Worlds of Race Revisited: A Meditation on Race in the Age of Obama." *Daedalus* 140, no. 1 (2011): 11–27.

Ellin, Abby. "Studying in the First Amendment, Playing Out on Campus." *New York Times*, June 22, 2016. https://medium.com/@UofCalifornia/its-time-to-free-speech-on-campus-again-8d58a24b6f79#.7a4t8u7y7.

Engberg, Mark E., and Sylvia Hurtado. "Developing Pluralistic Skills and Dispositions in College: Examining Racial/Ethnic Group Differences." *Journal of Higher Education* 82, no. 4 (July 2011): 416–443.

Erasmus, Desiderius. *The Education of a Christian Prince*. Ed. Lester Kruger Born. New York: Columbia University Press, 1936.

Faris, Robert, Amar Ashar, Urs Gasser, and Daisy Joo. *Understanding Harmful Speech Online*. Berkman Klein Center Research Publication no. 2016–21. Cambridge, MA: Berkman Klein Center, December 2016. doi:10.2139/ssrn.2882824.

Finkin, Matthew W., and Robert C. Post. *For the Common Good: Principles of American Academic Freedom*. New Haven, CT: Yale University Press, 2009.

First Amendment Center. *State of the First Amendment Survey Reports*. First Amendment Center at Vanderbilt University and the Newseum. http://www.firstamendmentcenter.org/sofa.

Fish, Stanley Eugene. *There's No Such Thing as Free Speech, and It's a Good Thing, Too*. New York: Oxford University Press, 1994.

Fish, Stanley Eugene. *Versions of Academic Freedom: From Professionalism to Revolution*. Chicago: University of Chicago Press, 2014.

Fitzpatrick, B. T. "The Diversity Lie." *Harvard Journal of Law and Public Policy* 27, no. 1 (Fall 2003): 385–397.

Foucault, Michel. *Fearless Speech*. Ed. Joseph Pearson. Los Angeles / Cambridge, MA: Semiotext(e) / distributed by MIT Press, 2001.

Foxman, Abraham H. *Viral Hate: Containing Its Spread on the Internet*. Ed. Christopher Wolf. New York: Palgrave Macmillan, 2013.

"Free Speech and the Academy." Special issue, *The New Criterion* 35, no. 5 (January 2017).

Furedi, Frank. *What's Happened to the University? A Sociological Exploration of Its Infantilisation*. Oxford: Routledge, 2017.

Gallup. "Confidence in Institutions." Gallup Historical Trends. June 2–7, 2015. http://www.gallup.com/poll/1597/confidence-institutions.aspx.

Garrison, William Lloyd, and William James Potter, recipient. "[Copy of letter to] Dear Mr. Potter [manuscript]." Boston, October 11, 1873.

Garton Ash, Timothy. *Free Speech: Ten Principles for a Connected World*. New Haven, CT: Yale University Press, 2016.

Gerber, S. D. "The Politics of Free Speech." *Social Philosophy & Policy* 21, no. 2 (Summer 2004): 23–47.

Gillman, Howard, and Erwin Chemerinsky. "Don't Mock or Ignore Students' Lack of Support for Free Speech. Teach Them." *Los Angeles Times*, March 31, 2016. http://www.latimes.com/opinion/op-ed/la-oe-chemerinsky-gillman-free-speech-on-campus-20160331-story.html.

Ginsberg, Jodie. "Global View: Universities Must Not Fear Offence and Controversy." *Index on Censorship* 44 (2015): 67–68.

Glass, Kimberly, Chris R. Glass, and R. J. Lynch. "Student Engagement and Affordances for Interaction with Diverse Peers: A Network Analysis." *Journal of Diversity in Higher Education* 9, no. 2 (June 2016): 170–187.

Goldsmith, Pat Antonio. "Schools' Role in Shaping Race Relations: Evidence on Friendliness and Conflict." *Social Problems* 51, no. 4 (2004): 587–612.

Graber, Mark A. *Transforming Free Speech: The Ambiguous Legacy of Civil Libertarianism*. Berkeley: University of California Press, 1991.

Greenawalt, Kent. *Fighting Words: Individuals, Communities, and Liberties of Speech*. Princeton, NJ: Princeton University Press, 1995.

Greenawalt, Kent. "Insults and Epithets: Are They Protected Speech?" *Rutgers Law Review* 42, no. 2 (1990): 287–307.

Greenawalt, Kent. *Speech, Crime, and the Uses of Language*. New York: Oxford University Press, 1989.

Grimké, Sarah Moore. *Letters on the Equality of the Sexes, and the Condition of Woman: Addressed to Mary S. Parker, President of the Boston Female Anti-Slavery Society*. Ed. Mary S. Parker. Boston: I. Knapp, 1838.

Gronke, Paul, and Timothy E. Cook. "Disdaining the Media: The American Public's Changing Attitudes toward the News." *Political Communication* 24, no. 3 (2007): 259–281.

Guinier, Lani. *The Tyranny of the Meritocracy: Democratizing Higher Education in America*. Boston: Beacon Press, 2015.

Gurin, Patricia, A. Nagda Biren Ratnesh, and Ximena Zuniga. *Dialogue across Difference: Practice, Theory, and Research on Intergroup Dialogue*. New York: Russell Sage Foundation, 2013.

Gurin, Patricia, A. Nagda Biren Ratnesh, and Ximena Zuniga. "Expert Report of Patricia Gurin (1999): Selections from the Compelling Need for Diversity in Higher Education, Expert Reports in Defense of the University of Michigan." *Equity & Excellence in Education* 32, no. 2 (July 9, 2006): 36–62.

Guyatt, Nicholas. *Bind Us Apart: How Enlightened Americans Invented Racial Segregation*. New York: Basic Books, 2016.

Haidt, Jonathan. *The Righteous Mind: Why Good People Are Divided by Politics and Religion*. New York: Pantheon Books, 2012.

Hamilton, Alexander, John Jay, James Madison, and E. H. Scott. *The Federalist and Other Constitutional Papers*. Chicago: Albert, Scott & Co., 1894.

Hammersley, Martyn. "Can Academic Freedom Be Justified? Reflections on the Arguments of Robert Post and Stanley Fish." *Higher Education Quarterly* 70, no. 2 (2016): 108–126.

Hare, Ivan, and James Weinstein. *Extreme Speech and Democracy*. Oxford: Oxford University Press, 2009.

Hart Research Associates. "2016 Survey of America's College Students." Conducted on Behalf of the Panetta Institute for Public Policy. http://www.panettainstitute.org/wp-content/uploads/Survey-report-2016.pdf.

Haynes, Charles C., and Association for Supervision and Curriculum Development. *The First Amendment In Schools: A Guide from the First Amendment Center*. Alexandria, VA: Association for Supervision and Curriculum Development (ASCD), 2003.

Healy, Thomas. *The Great Dissent: How Oliver Wendell Holmes Changed His Mind and Changed the History of Free Speech in America*. New York: Metropolitan Books, Henry Holt, 2013.

Higher Education Research Institute. "Findings from the 2015 Diverse Learning Environments Survey." Higher Education Research Institute, UCLA. http://www.heri.ucla.edu/briefs/DLE/DLE-2015-Brief.pdf.

Hughes, Geoffrey. *Political Correctness: A History of Semantics and Culture*. Chichester, UK / Malden, MA: Wiley-Blackwell, 2010.

Hurtado, S., and A. R. Alvarado. "Discrimination and Bias, Underrepresentation, and Sense of Belonging on Campus." Higher Education Research Institute, UCLA. http://www.heri.ucla.edu/PDFs/Discrimination-and-Bias-Underrepresentation-and-Sense-of-Belonging-on-Campus.pdf.

Hurtado, S., and R. Halualani. "Diversity Assessment, Accountability, and Action: Going beyond the Numbers." *Diversity and Democracy* 17, no. 4 (2014).

Hussar, William J., and Tabitha M. Bailey. *Projections of Education Statistics to 2023*. NCES 2013-008. Washington, DC: National Center for Education Statistics, 2016. https://nces.ed.gov/pubs2015/2015073.pdf.

Jacobs, Andrew T. "Restoring Free Speech and Liberty on Campus." *Teachers College Record* 108, no. 8 (August 2006): 1579–1582.

Jacobson, D. "The Academic Betrayal of Free Speech." *Social Philosophy & Policy* 21, no. 2 (Summer 2004): 48–80.

Jefferson, Thomas. *The Declaration of Independence*. Ed. Garnet Kindervater. London: Verso, 2007.

Jones, David R. "Declining Trust in Congress: Effects of Polarization and Consequences for Democracy." *Forum: A Journal of Applied Research in Contemporary Politics* 13, no. 3 (October 2015): 375–394.

Jorgensen, James D., and Lelia B. Helms. "Academic Freedom, the First Amendment and Competing Stakeholders: The Dynamics of a Changing Balance." *Review of Higher Education* 32, no. 1 (2008): 1–24.

Joughin, Louis. *Academic Freedom and Tenure: A Handbook of the American Association of University Professors*. Madison: University of Wisconsin Press, 1969.

Juhan, S. C. "Free Speech, Hate Speech, and the Hostile Speech Environment." *Virginia Law Review* 98, no. 7 (2012): 1577–1619.

Kagan, Elena. "Private Speech, Public Purpose: The Role of Governmental Motive in First Amendment Doctrine." *University of Chicago Law Review* 63, no. 2 (Spring 1996): 413–517.

Kamatali, Jean-Marie. "The Limits of the First Amendment: Protecting American Citizens' Free Speech in the Era of the Internet & the Global Marketplace of Ideas." *Wisconsin International Law Journal* 33, no. 4 (2016): 587–638.

Karran, Terence. "Academic Freedom: In Justification of a Universal Ideal." *Studies in Higher Education* 34, no. 3 (2009): 263–283.

Kena, G., W. Hussar, J. McFarland, C. de Brey, L. Musu-Gillette, X. Wang, J. Zhang, et al. *The Condition of Education 2016*. NCES 2016-144.

Washington, DC: National Center for Education Statistics, U.S. Department of Education, September 10, 2016. http://nces.ed.gov/pubs2016/2016144.pdf.

Kennedy, Randall. *Race, Crime, and the Law*. New York: Vintage Books, 1998.

Kent, E. A. "Free Speech on Campus." *Journal of Value Inquiry* 35, no. 4 (December 2001): 561–564.

Konrath, Sara H., Edward H. O'Brien, and Courtney Hsing. "Changes in Dispositional Empathy in American College Students over Time: A Meta-Analysis." *Personality and Social Psychology Review* 15, no. 2 (2011): 180–198.

Kors, Alan Charles. *The Shadow University: The Betrayal of Liberty on America's Campuses*. Ed. Harvey A. Silverglate. New York: Free Press, 1998.

Lane, Robert Wheeler. *Beyond the Schoolhouse Gate: Free Speech and the Inculcation of Values*. Philadelphia: Temple University Press, 1995.

Lee, Steven P. "Hate Speech in the Marketplace of Ideas." In *Freedom of Expression in a Diverse World*, AMINTAPHIL: The Philosophical Foundations of Law and Justice 3, ed. Deirdre Golash, 13–25. Dordrecht: Springer, 2010. doi: 10.1007/978-90-481-8999-1_2.

Lewis, Anthony. *Freedom for the Thought that We Hate: A Biography of the First Amendment*. New York: Basic Books, 2007.

Lewis, Earl, and Nancy Cantor. *Our Compelling Interests: The Value of Diversity for Democracy and a Prosperous Society*. Princeton, NJ: Princeton University Press, 2016.

Lopez, Mark Hugo, Peter Levine, Kenneth Dautrich, and David Yalof. "Schools, Education Policy, and the Future of the First Amendment." *Political Communication* 26, no. 1 (2009): 84–101. doi:10.1080/10584600802622910.

Lowery, J. W. "Restoring Free Speech and Liberty on Campus." *Review of Higher Education* 29, no. 3 (Spring 2006): 413–415.

Lukianoff, Greg. *Freedom from Speech*. New York: Encounter Books, 2014.

Lukianoff, Greg. *Unlearning Liberty: Campus Censorship and the End of American Debate*. New York: Encounter Books, 2012.

Macedo, Stephen. *Diversity and Distrust: Civic Education in a Multicultural Democracy*. Cambridge, MA: Harvard University Press, 2000.

Maitra, Ishani, and Mary Kathryn McGowan. *Speech and Harm: Controversies over Free Speech*. Oxford: Oxford University Press, 2012.

Mansilla, Veronica Boix. *Educating for Global Competence: Preparing Our Youth to Engage the World*. Ed. Anthony Jackson. Washington, DC: Asia Society, 2011.

Maranto, Robert, Richard E. Redding, Frederick M. Hess, and the American Enterprise Institute for Public Policy Research. *The Politically Correct University: Problems, Scope, and Reforms*. Washington, DC: AEI Press, 2009.

Martin, Georgianna L., and Christopher J. Broadhurst. *"Radical Academia?": Understanding the Climates for Campus Activists*. San Francisco: Jossey-Bass, 2014.

McEwan, Ian. *Nutshell: A Novel*. New York: Nan A. Talese / Doubleday, 2016.

McKitrick, Eric L. *Slavery Defended: The Views of the Old South*. Englewood Cliffs, NJ: Prentice-Hall, 1963.

Meiklejohn, Alexander. *Free Speech and Its Relation to Self-Government*. New York: Harper, 1948.

Menand, Louis. *The Future of Academic Freedom*. Chicago: University of Chicago Press, 1996.

Menand, Louis. *The Marketplace of Ideas*. New York: Norton, 2010.

Mill, John Stuart. *On Liberty: The Subjection of Women*. New York: Henry Holt, 1895.

Milton, John. *Areopagitica: A Speech of Mr. John Milton, for the Liberty of Unlicens'd Printing, to the Parliament of England*. London: N. Douglas, 1644.

Minow, Martha. *In Brown's Wake: Legacies of America's Educational Landmark*. New York: Oxford University Press, 2010.

Napolitano, Janet. "It's Time to Free Speech on Campus Again." *Medium*, October 12, 2016. https://medium.com/@UofCalifornia/its-time-to-free -speech-on-campus-again-8d58a24b6f79#.7a4t8u7y7.

Oltmann, Shannon M. "Intellectual Freedom and Freedom of Speech: Three Theoretical Perspectives." *Library Quarterly* 86, no. 2 (2016): 153–171.

O'Neil, Robert M. "Second Thoughts on the First Amendment in Higher Education." *Mississippi Law Journal* Symposium Edition on Education Law. *Mississippi Law Journal* 83, no. 4 (2014): 745–775.

Page, Scott E. *The Difference: How the Power of Diversity Creates Better Groups, Firms, Schools, and Societies*. Princeton, NJ: Princeton University Press, 2007.

Page, Scott E. *Diversity and Complexity*. Princeton, NJ: Princeton University Press, 2011.

Page, Scott E. "Where Diversity Comes from and Why It Matters?" *European Journal of Social Psychology* 44, no. 4 (2014): 267–279.

Patai, Daphne. "Ray Bradbury and the Assault on Free Thought." *Society* 50, no. 1 (February 2013): 41–47.

Peard, Thomas. "Is it Immoral to Prohibit Sexually Harassing Speech in the Classroom?" In *Freedom of Expression in a Diverse World*, AMINTA-PHIL: The Philosophical Foundations of Law and Justice 3, ed. Deirdre Golash, 75–85. Dordrecht: Springer, 2010. doi: 10.1007/978-90-481-8999-1_2.

Pettigrew, Thomas F. "Future Directions for Intergroup Contact Theory and Research." *International Journal of Intercultural Relations* 32, no. 3 (2008): 187–199.

Pettigrew, Thomas F., and Linda R. Tropp. "How Does Intergroup Contact Reduce Prejudice? Meta-Analytic Tests of Three Mediators." *European Journal of Social Psychology* 38, no. 6 (2008): 922–934. http://school-diversity.org/wp-content/uploads/2014/09/Tropp-written-testimony-for-New-York-City-Schools-12-2014.pdf.

Pew Research Center. *Beyond Distrust: How Americans View Their Government.* Washington, DC: Pew Research Center, November 23, 2015. http://www.people-press.org/2015/11/23/beyond-distrust-how-americans-view-their-government.

Pew Research Center. *Political Polarization in the American Public.* Washington, DC: Pew Research Center, June 12, 2014. http://www.people-press.org/files/2014/06/6-12-2014-Political-Polarization-Release.pdf.

Pew Research Center. *Social Media Conversations about Race.* Washington, DC: Pew Research Center, August 12, 2016. http://www.pewinternet.org/2016/08/15/social-media-conversations-about-race.

Pew Research Center. *On Views of Race and Inequality, Blacks and Whites Are Worlds Apart.* Washington, DC: Pew Research Center, June 27, 2016. http://www.pewsocialtrends.org/2016/06/27/on-views-of-race-and-inequality-blacks-and-whites-are-worlds-apart.

Popper, Karl R. *The Open Society and Its Enemies.* 5th ed. London: Routledge & Kegan Paul, 1966.

Post, Robert. *Democracy, Expertise, and Academic Freedom: A First Amendment Jurisprudence for the Modern State.* New Haven, CT: Yale University Press, 2012.

Post, Robert. "Participatory Democracy and Free Speech." *Virginia Law Review* 97, no. 3 (2011): 477–489.

Poushter, Jacob. *40% of Millennials OK with Limiting Speech Offensive to Minorities.* Washington, DC: Pew Research Center, November 20, 2015. http://www.pewresearch.org/fact-tank/2015/11/20/40-of-millennials-ok-with-limiting-speech-offensive-to-minorities.

Prakash, Aseem, and Matthew Potoski. "Dysfunctional Institutions? Toward a New Agenda in Governance Studies." *Regulation & Governance* 10, no. 2 (June 2016): 115–125.

Putnam, Robert D. *Bowling Alone: The Collapse and Revival of American Community*. New York: Simon & Schuster, 2000.

Putnam, Robert D. "E Pluribus Unum: Diversity and Community in the Twenty-First Century—The 2006 Johan Skytte Prize Lecture." *Scandinavian Political Studies* 30, no. 2 (2007): 137–174.

Rabban, David M. *Free Speech in Its Forgotten Years*. Cambridge: Cambridge University Press, 1997.

Rahn, Wendy M., and John E. Transue. "Social Trust and Value Change: The Decline of Social Capital in American Youth, 1976–1995." *Political Psychology* 19, no. 3 (1998): 545–565.

Rauch, Jonathan. *Kindly Inquisitors: The New Attacks on Free Thought*. Expanded ed. Chicago: University of Chicago Press, 2013.

Renard, John. *Fighting Words: Religion, Violence, and the Interpretation of Sacred Texts*. Berkeley: University of California Press, 2012.

Ross, Catherine J. *Lessons in Censorship: How Schools and Courts Subvert Students' First Amendment Rights*. Cambridge, MA: Harvard University Press, 2015.

Ross, Lauren. "Pursuing Academic Freedom after *Garcetti v. Ceballos*." *Texas Law Review* 91, no. 5 (2013): 1253–1281.

Rothman, Stanley, April Kelly-Woessner, and Matthew Woessner. *The Still Divided Academy: How Competing Visions of Power, Politics, and Diversity Complicate the Mission of Higher Education*. Lanham, MD: Rowman and Littlefield, 2010.

Sarabyn, Kelly. "Free Speech at Private Universities." *Journal of Law & Education* 39, no. 2 (2010): 145–182.

Saunders, Tom. "The Limits on University Control of Graduate Student Speech." *Yale Law Journal* 112, no. 5 (2003): 1295–1302.

Scanlon, T. M. *A Theory of Freedom of Expression.* Cambridge: Cambridge University Press, 2003.

Schauer, Frederick. "On the Distinction between Speech and Action." *Emory Law Journal* 65, no. 2 (2015): 427–454.

Scott, Joan Wallach. "Restoring Free Speech and Liberty on Campus / FIRE's Guide to Free Speech on Campus." *Academe* 91, no. 6 (November 2005): 62–66.

Sidanius, Jim. *The Diversity Challenge: Social Identity and Intergroup Relations on the College Campus.* New York: Russell Sage Foundation, 2008.

Silverglate, Harvey A., David French, and Greg Lukianoff. *FIRE's Guide to Free Speech on Campus. FIRE's Guides to Student Rights on Campus.* 2nd ed. Philadelphia: Foundation for Individual Rights in Education, 2012. http://files.eric.ed.gov/fulltext/ED536994.pdf.

Smith, Bruce L. R., Jeremy D. Mayer, and A. Lee Fritschler. *Closed Minds?: Politics and Ideology in American Universities.* Washington, DC: Brookings Institution Press, 2008.

Sorial, Sarah, and Catriona Mackenzie. "The Limits of the Public Sphere: The Advocacy of Violence." *Critical Horizons* 12, no. 2 (2011): 165–188.

Steele, Claude. *Whistling Vivaldi: And Other Clues to How Stereotypes Affect Us.* New York: Norton, 2010.

Stevenson, Bryan. *Just Mercy: A Story of Justice and Redemption.* New York: Spiegel & Grau, 2014.

Stone, Geoffrey R. *Perilous Times: Free Speech in Wartime from the Sedition Act of 1798 to the War on Terrorism.* New York: Norton, 2004.

Stone, Geoffrey R., and Mark V. Tushnet. *The First Amendment.* 2nd ed. New York: Aspen Publishers, 2003.

Sullivan, Kathleen M. "Two Concepts of Freedom of Speech." *Harvard Law Review* 124, no. 1 (2010): 143–177.

Sullivan, Kathleen M. "Women, Speech and Experience." *The Good Society* 14, nos. 1–2 (2005): 35–39.

Sunstein, Cass R. *Democracy and the Problem of Free Speech*. New York: Free Press, 1993.

Sunstein, Cass R. *Designing Democracy: What Constitutions Do*. Oxford: Oxford University Press, 2001.

Sunstein, Cass R. *Going to Extremes: How Like Minds Unite and Divide*. Oxford: Oxford University Press, 2009.

Sunstein, Cass R. "Liberalism, Speech Codes, and Related Problems." *Academe* 79, no. 4 (1993): 14–25.

Tanner, Lauren E. "Rights and Regulations: Academic Freedom and a University's Right to Regulate the Student Press." *Texas Law Review* 86, no. 2 (2007): 421–450.

Tatum, Beverly Daniel. *Why Are All the Black Kids Sitting Together in the Cafeteria? And Other Conversations about Race*. New York: Basic Books, 2003.

Ten Cate, Irene M. "Speech, Truth, and Freedom: An Examination of John Stuart Mill's and Justice Oliver Wendell Holmes's Free Speech Defenses." *Yale Journal of Law & the Humanities* 22 (2010): 35–81.

Thomas, John L. *Slavery Attacked: The Abolitionist Crusade*. Englewood Cliffs, NJ: Prentice-Hall, 1965.

Toma, J. Douglas. "Academic Freedom at the Dawn of a New Century: How Terrorism, Governments, and Culture Wars Impact Free Speech." *Journal of Higher Education* 79, no. 4 (July August 2008): 482–484.

Tribe, Laurence H. *American Constitutional Law*. 2nd ed. New York: Foundation Press, 1988.

Tropp, Linda R. "Benefits of Contact between Racial and Ethnic Groups: A Summary of Research Findings." Testimony in Support of New York City School Diversity Bills, Hearing on Diversity in New York City Schools, December 11, 2014. http://school-diversity.org/wp-content/uploads/2014/09/Tropp-written-testimony-for-New-York-City-Schools-12-2014.pdf.

Tropp, Linda R., and Thomas F. Pettigrew. "Relationships between Intergroup Contact and Prejudice among Minority and Majority Status Groups." *Psychological Science* 16, no. 12 (2005): 951–957.

Twenge, Jean M., W. K. Campbell, and Nathan T. Carter. "Declines in Trust in Others and Confidence in Institutions among American Adults and Late Adolescents, 1972–2012." *Psychological Science* 25, no. 10 (2014): 1914–1923.

Twenge, Jean M., Nathan T. Carter, and W. K. Campbell. "Time Period, Generational, and Age Differences in Tolerance for Controversial Beliefs and Lifestyles in the United States, 1972–2012." *Social Forces* 94, no. 1 (2015): 379–399.

Twenge, Jean M., Julie J. Exline, Joshua B. Grubbs, Ramya Sastry, and W. Keith Campbell. "Generational and Time Period Differences in American Adolescents' Religious Orientation, 1966–2014." *PLoS One* 10, no. 5 (2015): e0121454.

Unger, Roberto Mangabeira. *Democracy Realized: The Progressive Alternative*. London: Verso, 1998.

U.S. Congress House Committee on the Judiciary Subcommittee on the Constitution and Civil Justice. *First Amendment Protections on Public College and University Campuses: Hearing before the Subcommittee on the Constitution and Civil Justice of the Committee on the Judiciary, House of Representatives, One Hundred Fourteenth Congress, First Session, June 2, 2015*. Washington, DC: U.S. Government Publishing Office, 2015.

Waldron, Jeremy. *The Harm in Hate Speech*. Cambridge, MA: Harvard University Press, 2012.

Weeks, Rory Allen. "The First Amendment, Public School Students, and the Need for Clear Limits on School Officials' Authority over Off-Campus Student Speech." *Georgia Law Review* 46, no. 4 (Summer 2012): 1157–1193.

Weinstein, James. *Hate Speech, Pornography, and the Radical Attack on Free Speech Doctrine*. Boulder, CO: Westview Press, 1999.

Wendel, W. B. "A Moderate Defense of Hate Speech Regulations on University Campuses." *Harvard Journal on Legislation* 41, no. 2 (Summer 2004): 407–420.

Wildavsky, Rachel, and Erin O'Connor. *Free to Teach, Free to Learn: Understanding and Maintaining Academic Freedom in Higher Education.* Washington, DC: American Council of Trustees and Alumni, April 2013.

Williams, Joanna. *Academic Freedom in an Age of Conformity: Confronting the Fear of Knowledge.* New York: Palgrave Macmillan, 2016.

Winkle-Wagner, Rachelle, and Angela M. Locks. *Diversity and Inclusion on Campus: Supporting Racially and Ethnically Underrepresented Students.* New York: Routledge, 2013.

Wolff, Robert Paul. *A Critique of Pure Tolerance.* Ed. Herbert Marcuse and Barrington Moore. Boston: Beacon Press, 1965.

Yong, Caleb. "Does Freedom of Speech Include Hate Speech?" *Res Publica: A Journal of Moral, Legal and Political Philosophy* 17, no. 4 (2011): 385–403.

Index